Foreword

It may not be immediately obvious what surface water drainage has to do with the UK's commitment to sustainable development, but I request just a few minutes of your time to consider this.

There are many challenges that face us as we enter the new millennium, not least the demand for new housing and industrial development in Scotland and Northern Ireland. In line with our commitment to sustainable development, it is becoming increasingly important to turn the concept into reality and find sustainable ways to service new developments.

One of the difficulties that needs to be resolved for any new development is the drainage of surface water without causing flooding or pollution, and without sterilising valuable development land. This design manual is the first authoritative document to provide detailed technical advice on sustainable methods of surface water drainage in the UK. This manual puts sustainable development into practice.

Sustainable urban drainage systems (SUDS) must not be an add-on at the end, but should be at the heart of the design process. This design manual makes it plain that a multi-disciplinary approach to design is required, and involves developers, drainage engineers, planners, architects, landscape architects, ecologists and hydrologists. All these professionals need to work in partnership with each other, and the statutory authorities, in order to design sustainable surface water drainage systems that take into account water quantity, water quality and the amenity value of the development.

As part of that partnership approach, I am delighted that the Scottish water authorities and Scottish local authorities have reached agreement on the maintenance of shared public SUDS. The water authorities will maintain below-ground facilities and the local authorities the above-ground ones. This agreement, on which I congratulate all concerned, comes into effect for two years from the publication of this manual, after which it will be reviewed with the intention that the partnership is continued into the future.

It has been said that sustainable development is "a journey and not a destination", and this design manual should be seen in this light. It will be refined on the basis of experience and good practice at sites across Scotland and Northern Ireland. It will be the ongoing task of the Sustainable Urban Drainage Scottish Working Party to oversee this process in Scotland.

I commend this design manual to you and trust that it leaves you in no doubt that surface water drainage systems can be designed in a manner that makes an invaluable contribution to sustainable development.

Sir Fraser Morrison
Morrison Construction Group

Contents

Conventional surface water drainage techniques can cause flooding and pollution and disrupt the water cycle – to the detriment of water resources and the natural environment. A different approach is needed to reach a more sustainable solution. This manual describes current best design practice in Scotland and Northern Ireland and sets out the technical and planning considerations for designing sustainable urban drainage systems (SUDS) for surface water. Drainage methods inspired by natural processes are introduced, and guidance is given on how the design team should select and design a suitable system.

Urban drainage systems can add value to the built environment

This section explains why urban areas need to be drained and how sustainable urban drainage systems can provide a better approach for surface water management than traditional practices.

Various methods of managing surface water runoff have common properties. This overview of some of the available techniques describes the practical aspects of each group.

The stages of a typical development are described in this section. It discusses the responsibilities of all parties involved in developing a drainage system and sets out the statutory framework for Scotland.

CIRIA C521

CIRIA C521

London 2000

Sustainable urban drainage systems

design manual for Scotland and Northern Ireland

WORKING PARTY

suds

SUSTAINABLE URBAN DRAINAGE SCOTTISH WORKING PARTY

CIRIA

sharing knowledge
■
building best practice

Acknowledgements

This manual is one of the outputs of CIRIA Research Project 555, "Sustainable urban drainage systems". CIRIA's research contractor for this part of the project was Binnie Black and Veatch in association with Coventry University and Sir Frederick Snow and Partners (Scotland) Ltd.

The manual was written by Peter Martin, Bridget Turner and Kate Waddington of Binnie Black & Veatch; Chris Pratt of Coventry University; Neil Campbell of Sir Frederick Snow and Partners (Scotland) Ltd; Judy Payne and Brian Reed of CIRIA and members of the steering group.

CIRIA wishes to acknowledge contributions made by Larry Roesner (Camp Dresser and McKee/ University of Abertay), David Macdonald (Binnie Black and Veatch) and Bob Bray (Robert Bray Associates).

Funding for the manual was provided by SNIFFER (Scotland and Northern Ireland Forum for Environmental Research) SEPA and the Scottish Water Authorities.

Production of this manual was guided by a steering group, chaired by Colin Bayes of the Scottish Environment Protection Agency (SEPA), consisting of:

Jim Conlin (East of Scotland Water)
Ian Corner (SEPA)
Brian D'Arcy (SEPA)
Tom Docherty (T Docherty Ltd)
Sarah Gillman (SEPA)
Phillip Gilmour (Scottish Executive)
Karen Heywood (Scottish Society of Directors of Planning, representing the Convention of Scottish Local Authorities)
Forbes Macgregor (Scottish Executive)
John McMurchie (West of Scotland Water)
Eddie McMurray (Scottish Housebuilders' Association)
Jock Maxwell (Meedhurst Project Management)
Graeme Rose (SEPA)
Martin Squibbs (North of Scotland Water Authority)
John Toole (Society of Chief Officers of Transportation in Scotland, representing Convention of Scottish Local Authorities)
John Watson (Lanarkshire Development Agency)
Tom Williamson (Scottish Executive)

Photographs

Pages iv, v, 2, 9, 10, 11, 27, 36, 40, 44, 68, 83, 84, 93 courtesy of SEPA
Pages 5, 41, 61 courtesy of Meedhurst Project Management
Pages 8, 46, 74, 75 courtesy of University of Abertay, Dundee
Pages 14 (top), 18, 28, 38, 47, 63, 73, 88, 91 courtesy of Binnie Black & Veatch
Page 14 (bottom) courtesy of Wilcon Homes
Page 65 courtesy of Formpave
Page 81 courtesy of Bovis
Page 84 courtesy of the Environment Agency

Other photographs supplied by steering group members and organisations not named above are also gratefully acknowledged.

Cover photograph courtesy of SEPA

Additional support was given by the UK steering group for CIRIA Research Project 555, colleagues of steering group members and the following correspondents:

Philip Anderson (Scottish Executive)
Chris Jefferies (University of Abertay Dundee)
Ray Bennett (Northern Ireland Environment and Heritage Service)
Craig Berry (WA Fairhurst and Partners)
Jonathan Chapman (Environment Agency)
Frank Guz (Dundee City Council)
Mike Harrison (Health and Safety Executive)
Ian Herd (Scottish Executive)
Iain Ross (Scottish Association of Chief Building Control Officers (SACBO))
Ruth Wolstenholme (SNIFFER)

CIRIA C521

Drainage devices have to be carefully designed and built in order to work successfully

4 Selecting SUDS

This is a technical chapter, aimed at designers. It describes how to agree a set of design criteria and presents a framework for the design team to select a drainage system.

It also sets out some of the other considerations that the design team should review while designing its system.

5 Designing SUDS

Technical guidance is given on a variety of drainage techniques. This covers construction and maintenance issues as well as some of the factors that the design team will need to address as the drainage system is developed.

Appendices

This manual addresses the technical issues surrounding urban drainage systems being developed in Scotland and Northern Ireland. A companion volume (C522) discusses the technical issues in England and Wales. The wider aspects are covered in more detail in Sustainable urban drainage systems – best practice (C523). Promotional brochures are available from SEPA.

Key guidelines

Throughout this manual the recommendations of the Sustainable Urban Drainage Scottish Working Party (SUDSWP) have been highlighted for ease of reference.

0

Glossary: technical expressions are explained throughout the document.

This manual has been written with respect to existing Scottish legislation. Some of the relevant legislation and guidance is:

- Building (Scotland) Acts 1959, together with the relevant technical standards
- Sewerage (Scotland) Act 1968 (as amended)
- Local Government Scotland Acts 1973 and 1994
- Control of Pollution Act 1974 (as amended)
- Roads (Scotland) Act 1984
- Environment Act 1995
- Flood Prevention and Land Drainage (Scotland) Act 1997
- Town and Country Planning (Scotland) Act 1997
- NPPG7 *Planning and flooding* gives policy guidance.

Glossary

Attenuation	Increase in duration of flow hydrograph with a consequent reduction in peak flow.
Baffle	A device designed to prevent flows short circuiting through a pond.
Balancing pond	A pond designed to attenuate flows by storing runoff during peak periods and releasing it after the flood peak has passed.
Basin	Flow control or water treatment structure that is normally dry.
Catchment	The area contributing flow to a point on a drainage system.
Catchpit	A small chamber incorporating a sediment collection sump which the runoff flows through.
Combined sewer	A sewer designed to carry foul sewage and surface runoff in the same pipe.
Curtilage	Land area within property boundaries.
Design criteria	A set of standards agreed by the developer, planners and regulators that the proposed system should satisfy.
Detention basin	A basin constructed to store water temporarily to attenuate flows.
Dry	Free of water under dry weather flow conditions.
Environmental management plan	A management agreement for an area or project set up in order to make sure the declared management objectives for the area or project are met. EMPs are often undertaken as part of an environmental impact assessment and are set out in several stages with responsibilities clearly set down and environmental monitoring in place to show compliance with the plan.
Extended detention basin	A detention basin where the runoff is stored beyond the time for attenuation. The extra time allows natural processes to remove some of the pollutants in the water.
Filter drain	A linear drain consisting of a trench filled with a permeable material, often with a perforated pipe in the base of the trench to assist drainage.
First flush	Runoff from a site will wash pollutants off the surface; this may be near the beginning of the flow from a small uniform catchment, but on large catchments the pollutants might not be in the initial flow.
Flood frequency	The probability of a flowrate being exceeded in any year.
Floodplain	Land adjacent to a river which is subject to regular flooding.

Infiltration – to the ground	The passage of surface water through the surface of the ground.
Infiltration – to a sewer	The entry of groundwater to a sewer.
Infiltration basin	A dry basin designed to promote infiltration of surface water to the ground.
Infiltration trench	A trench, usually filled with stone, designed to promote infiltration of surface water to the ground.
Interflow	Shallow infiltration to the soil, from where it may infiltrate vertically to an aquifer, move horizontally to a watercourse or be stored and subsequently evaporated.
Lagoon	A pond designed for the settlement of suspended solids.
Offstream	Dry weather flow bypasses the storage area.
Onstream	Dry weather flow passes through the storage area.
Permeable pavement	A permeable surface that is paved and drains through voids between solid parts of the pavement.
Permeable surface	Surface designed to promote infiltration of surface runoff into a permeable sub-base, before disposal.
Pond	Flow control or water treatment structure that is wet.
Porous paving	A permeable surface that drains through voids that are integral to the pavement.
Pound	A section of a swale designed to detain runoff.
Recurrence interval	The average time between runoff events that have a certain flow rate, eg a flow of 2 m/s might have a recurrence interval of two years.
Retention pond	A pond where runoff is detained for several days to allow settlement and biological treatment of some pollutants.
RoSPA	Royal Society for the Prevention of Accidents.
Runoff	Water that flows over the ground surface to the drainage system. This occurs if the ground is impermeable or if permeable ground is saturated.
SEPA	Scottish Environment Protection Agency.
Separate sewer	A sewer for surface water or foul sewage, but not a combination of both.
SNH	Scottish Natural Heritage.
Soakaway	A subsurface structure into which surface water is conveyed, designed to promote infiltration.
Source control	The control of runoff at or near its source.

Sub-base	A layer of material on the sub-grade that provides a foundation for a pavement surface.
Sub-catchment	A division of a catchment, to allow runoff to be managed as near to the source as is reasonable.
Sub-grade	Surface of an excavation prepared to support a pavement.
Subsidiarity	The principle that an issue should be managed as close as is reasonable to its source.
SUDS	Sustainable urban drainage system; a sequence of management practices and control structures designed to drain surface water in a more sustainable fashion than some conventional techniques.
Surface water management train	The management of runoff in stages as it drains from a site.
Swale	A grass-lined channel designed to drain water from a site as well as controlling the flow and quality of the surface water.
Treatment volume	The volume of surface runoff that contains the most polluted portion of the flow from a storm.
Watercourse	Any natural or artificial channel that conveys surface water.
Way leave	A right of access to the route of a pipeline crossing privately owned land.
Wet	Containing water under dry weather flow conditions.
Wetland	A pond that has a high proportion of emergent vegetation in relation to open water.

1 Introducing SUDS

Sustainable urban drainage is a concept that focuses decisions about drainage on the environment and on people. It takes account of the quantity and quality of runoff, and the amenity value of surface water in the urban environment. Many existing urban drainage systems are damaging to the environment and are not sustainable in the long term.

Sustainable development and Agenda 21

It has long been recognised that there can be conflict between economic development and protection of the environment. Sustainable development has social, economic and environmental implications.

Sustainable development was the central theme of the UN Earth Summit at Rio de Janeiro in 1992, which called on governments to produce their own strategies for sustainable development. The UK government updated its national strategy in May 1999. Parallel to this, the Local Government Management Board published *Local Agenda 21 – a framework for local sustainability*. Local authorities all have their own Agenda 21 strategies.

Cities, towns and villages create demands on the environment by using resources and producing waste. The built environment is therefore one area where the strategies of sustainable development should be put into practice.

Urban drainage

Any built-up area will need to be drained to remove excess surface water. Traditionally this has been done using underground pipe systems designed for **quantity**, to prevent flooding locally by conveying the water away as quickly as possible. The alteration of natural flow patterns can lead to problems elsewhere in the catchment. More recently, water **quality** issues have become important, due to pollutants from urban areas being washed into rivers or the groundwater, where it is difficult to remove them. Traditional drainage systems cannot easily control poor runoff quality and may contribute to the problem. The **amenity** aspects, such as water resources, community facilities, landscaping potential and provision of varied wildlife habitats have largely been ignored. Current drainage systems are not designed with these wider considerations in mind. Continuing to drain built-up areas with limited objectives and ignoring wider issues is not a sustainable long-term option.

Amenity: many issues are affected by the way surface water is managed. These include the landscape, land use, wildlife habitats, land values, recreation opportunities and water resources. Opportunity costs, perceptions of risk and construction impact should also be considered when designing drainage systems. All these environmental and community issues have been gathered together under the heading of amenity.

Drainage systems can be designed for attenuation, treatment and amenity

Drainage systems can be developed in line with the ideals of sustainable development, by balancing the various issues that should be influencing the design. Surface water drainage methods that take account of quantity, quality and amenity issues are collectively referred to as sustainable urban drainage systems (SUDS – see diagram below). These systems are more sustainable than traditional drainage methods because they:

♦ protect or enhance water quality

♦ are sympathetic to the environmental setting and the needs of the local community

♦ provide a habitat for wildlife in urban watercourses

♦ encourage natural groundwater recharge (where appropriate).

They do this by:

♦ dealing with runoff close to where the rain falls

♦ managing potential flooding at its source, now and in the future

♦ protecting water resources from point pollution (such as accidental spills) and diffuse pollution.

They also may allow new development in areas where existing sewerage systems are close to full capacity, therefore enabling development within existing urban areas.

This manual addresses the design issues on a local level. For further exploration of the catchment-wide planning, economic, social and technical matters see *Sustainable urban drainage systems – best practice (CIRIA C523)*.

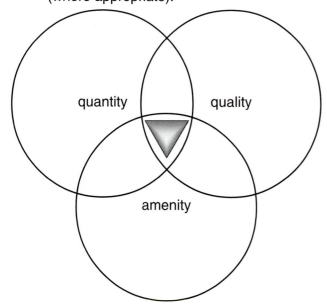

The urban drainage triangle – balancing the impact of urban drainage on the environment

Sustainable urban drainage

SUDS are made up of one or more structures built to manage surface water runoff. They are used in conjunction with good management of the site, to prevent pollution. There are four general methods of control:

- filter strips and swales

- filter drains and permeable surfaces

- infiltration devices

- basins and ponds.

The controls should be located as close as possible to where the rainwater falls, providing **attenuation** for the runoff. They also provide varying degrees of treatment for surface water, using the natural processes of sedimentation, filtration, adsorption and biological degradation.

> **Attenuation:** slowing down the rate of flow to prevent flooding and erosion, with a consequent increase in the duration of the flow.

SUDS can be designed to fit into most urban settings, from hard-surfaced areas to soft landscaped features. The variety of design options available allows designers and planners to consider local land use, land take, future **management** and the needs of local people when undertaking the drainage design, going beyond simple drainage and flood control. The range of options means that active decisions have to be made that balance the wishes of different stakeholders and the risks associated with each option.

> **Management issues** are often a barrier to successful implementation of SUDS. These should be resolved during the planning stage and are discussed in detail in Chapter 3.

Management train

A useful concept used in the development of drainage systems is the **surface water management train**. Just as in a natural catchment, drainage techniques can be used in series to change the flow and quality characteristics of the runoff in stages.

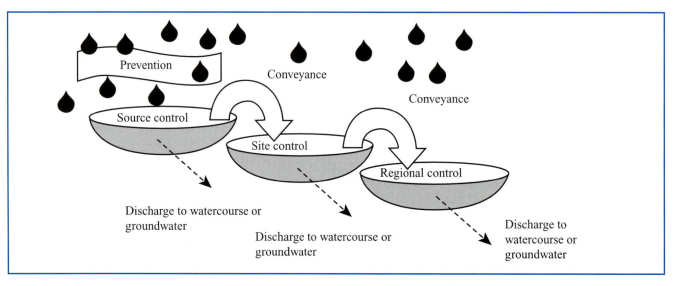

Surface water management train: addressing runoff quantity and quality at all stages of the drainage system

The management train starts with prevention, or good housekeeping measures, for individual premises; and progresses through local **source controls** to larger downstream **site** and **regional controls**. Runoff need not pass through all the stages in the management train. It could flow straight to a site control, but as a general principle it is better to deal with it as locally as possible, returning the water to the natural drainage system as near to the source as possible. This supports the environmental principle of **subsidiarity**.

> **Source control:** the control of runoff at or near its source.
>
> **Site** and **regional controls** manage runoff drained from several sub-catchments. The controls deal with runoff on a catchment scale rather than at source.

> **Subsidiarity:** the principle that an issue should be managed as close as possible to its source.

The management train concept promotes division of the area to be drained into **sub-catchments** with different drainage characteristics and land uses, each with its own drainage strategy. Dealing with the water locally not only reduces the quantity that has to be managed at any one point, but also reduces the need for **conveying** the water off the site.

Conveyance: the main purpose of drainage systems is to manage the excess surface water that results from developing a greenfield site. If the water cannot be dealt with on site, it will have to be drained away to a point where it can acceptably return to the natural water cycle.

Sub-catchment: a small area within a larger development that can be individually drained.

Drainage systems work in series: here a settling pond to take out coarse sediments is followed by a filter strip to treat the runoff further; the runoff is polished in a wetland before returning to the environment

When dividing catchments into small sections it is important to retain a perspective on how this affects the whole catchment management and the hydrological cycle. The role of SUDS outwith the immediate limits of a development site is discussed more fully in *Sustainable urban drainage systems – best practice* (CIRIA C523).

2 Using SUDS

The techniques used in SUDS can be grouped into four general methods of control: filter strips and swales, filter drains and permeable surfaces, infiltration devices, and basins and ponds. This section describes each method of control in terms of how it works, basic design considerations, and practical details.

The hydrological cycle

Sustainable urban drainage systems make use of natural drainage processes. An understanding of the hydrological cycle will enable designers to design drainage systems in harmony with the environment.

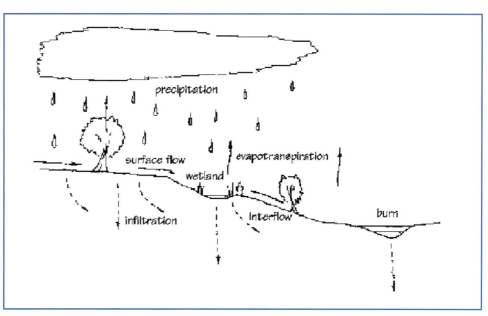

The hydrological cycle is a complex system of water flows

An integrated system

SUDS do not operate as a series of isolated drainage devices, but should be designed and operated holistically. Each component adds to the performance of the whole drainage system. The range of options available allows the surface water to be drained in a variety of equally acceptable ways.

The types of device described below indicate the scope of drainage systems. The definitions are not rigorous, as each device may operate in several ways: attenuating, treating and disposing of the surface water to a greater or lesser extent, depending on the details of the design.

SUDS techniques work in the same way as natural processes

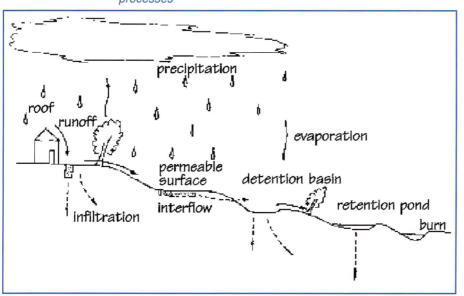

Filter strips and swales

What are they?

Filter strips and swales are vegetated surface features that drain water evenly off impermeable areas. Swales are long shallow channels whereas filter strips are gently sloping areas of ground.

Swales can be integrated into the landscaping of a development

How they work

Both devices mimic natural drainage patterns by allowing rainwater to run in sheets through vegetation, slowing and filtering the flow. Swales can also be designed for a combination of conveyance, infiltration, detention and treatment of runoff.

Quantity

Swales are usually designed as conveyance systems, but can also incorporate check dams to increase attenuation and, where applicable, infiltration. Filter strips only attenuate the flow slightly, but they can be used to reduce the drained impermeable area.

Quality

Swales and filter strips are effective at removing polluting solids through filtration and sedimentation. The vegetation traps organic and mineral particles that are then incorporated into the soil, while the vegetation takes up any nutrients.

Amenity

Swales and filter strips are often integrated into the surrounding land use, for example public open space or road verges. Local wild grass and flower species can be introduced for visual interest and to provide a wildlife habitat. Care should be taken in the choice of vegetation as tussocks create local eddies, increasing the potential for erosion on slopes. Shrubs and trees can be planted, but in this case the vegetated area will need to be wider and have a gentler slope.

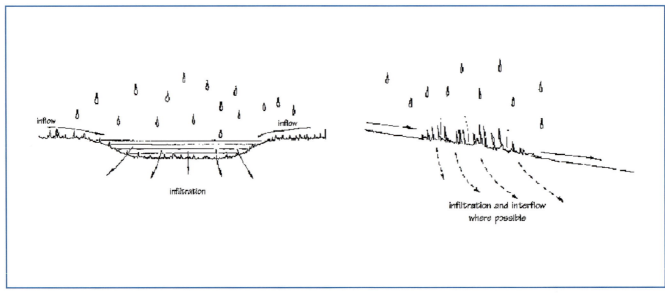

Swales convey runoff along the channel   *Filter strips treat surface flows*

Design

Swales and filter strips are particularly suitable for treatment of runoff from small residential developments, parking areas and roads. For maximum effectiveness, surface water runoff should flow in sheets down the side of the swale or across the filter strip. The development of this sheet flow is important to avoid erosion and maximise filtration of the runoff. The flow depth should be less than the height of the grass to ensure filtration. Piping surface water to a swale or filter strip is not recommended.

Care should be taken to establish sheet flow down the sides of a swale or across a filter strip

Construction

Swales and filter strips are landscape features, with smooth surfaces and a gentle downhill gradient. Vegetation should be planted during the growing season, and alternative arrangements made for the management of surface water drainage until the vegetation is established. The soil should not be compacted during construction.

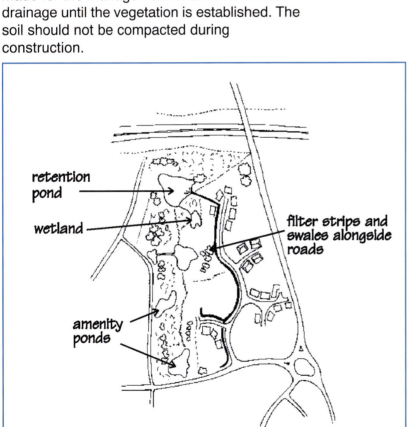

Green corridors act as public open space and provide visual, drainage and wildlife links through a development

Operation

Apart from regular mowing, clearing litter and periodic removal of excess silt, filter strips and swales require little maintenance. They should be inspected after severe storms for litter and signs of erosion.

Filter drains and permeable surfaces

What are they?

Filter drains and permeable surfaces are devices that have a volume of permeable material below ground to store surface water. Runoff flows to this storage area via a permeable surface. This can include:

◆ grass (if the area will not be trafficked)

◆ reinforced grass

◆ gravelled areas

◆ solid paving blocks with large vertical holes filled with soil or gravel

◆ solid paving blocks with gaps between the individual units

◆ porous paving blocks with a system of voids within the unit

◆ continuous surfaces with an inherent system of voids.

Filter drains are linear devices that drain water off an impermeable surface in a diffuse manner. Permeable surfaces act by directly intercepting the rain where it falls, so are true source controls. They are currently used for car parks, residential driveways, paths and patios, but not for adoptable roads and footpaths.

How they work

The water passes through the surface to the permeable fill. This allows the storage, treatment, transport and infiltration of water. Both the surface and the sub-base of a pavement must allow the passage of water – for this reason, porous asphalt laid on a traditional impermeable base is not a permeable pavement.

Filter drains can be used as robust drainage for roads

Quantity
The amount of water stored depends on the voids ratio of the permeable fill or sub-base, the plan area and depth. Water can be disposed of by infiltration, an underdrain, or pumped out. Overflow can be via a high level drain or controlled surface flow. In some situations the water should not be stored for extended periods because it can affect the strength of the surrounding soil.

Quality
The permeable fill or sub-base traps sediment, thereby cleaning up runoff. Recent research shows that they also provide some treatment for other pollutants, such as oil.

Amenity
The variety of surfaces is wide enough for the landscape architect to select a hard landscape style to suit the style of the development. By their nature, filter drains and permeable surfaces ensure an efficient use of space.

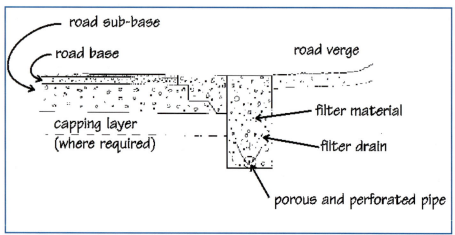
Cross-section through a filter drain

Permeable surfaces can look like conventional paved areas

Operation

The surface should be kept clear of silt and cleaned at least twice a year to keep the voids clear. The use of grit and salt will adversely affect the treatment and drainage potential of the pavement but should not often be needed, because ice is less likely to form on the surface. The control of weeds will have to be managed carefully as weed-killers may disrupt the biological action in the sub-base.

Users of the area should be made aware of the drainage system and encouraged to treat the pavement appropriately.

Major maintenance might be required to re-establish the drainage characteristics of the system, to remove silt and other trapped contaminants. The frequency and level of work required will depend on the day-to-day treatment and operation of the permeable surface.

Design

The roads authority may offer guidance on filter drains, and there is a wide range of manufacturers' literature to aid the design of permeable surfaces. The surfacing type should suit the intended use – the surface, sub-base and sub-grade should all have sufficient structural strength to cope with the loads resulting from construction and the expected traffic use.

If runoff is disposed of by infiltration, care should be taken to ensure that the supporting soil will retain its strength when saturated.

Ideally the device should be laid fairly flat, so that runoff enters the pavement evenly and water flows slowly through the sub-base by gravity.

The surface should be permeable enough to cope with the design rainfall intensity. Just as overland flow will occur on sandy soils during extreme rainfall events, flooding and runoff will occur on permeable surfaces when the rainfall exceeds the infiltration rate of the surface or the storage capacity provided in the fill or sub-base.

*Gravel surfaces do not interrupt
the natural flow of rain water*

Construction

Construction of the surface courses should be faster than conventional techniques as there is no need to lay the surface to a complex pattern of falls and there are no gullies or manholes to work around. The area should be protected to prevent sand and silt from construction blocking the voids in a permeable surface.

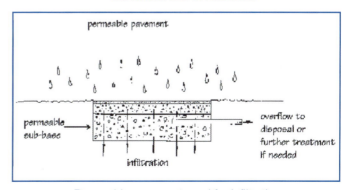

Permeable pavement used for infiltration

Infiltration devices

What are they?

Infiltration devices drain water directly into the ground. They may be used at source or the runoff can be conveyed in a pipe or swale to the infiltration area. They include soakaways, infiltration trenches and infiltration basins as well as swales, filter drains and ponds. Infiltration devices can be integrated into and form part of the landscaped areas.

Soakaways and infiltration trenches are completely below ground, and water should not appear on the surface. Infiltration basins and swales for infiltration store water on the ground surface, but are dry except in periods of heavy rainfall.

Inlet to an infiltration trench

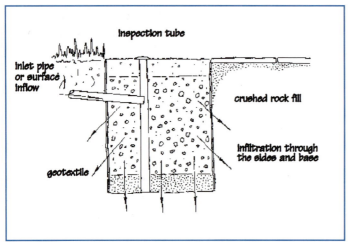

Cross-section through a traditional soakaway

How they work

Infiltration devices work by enhancing the natural capacity of the ground to store and drain water. Rain falling onto permeable (eg sandy) soil soaks into it. Infiltration devices use this natural process to dispose of surface water runoff. Limitations occur where the soil is not very permeable, the water table is shallow or the groundwater quality under the site might be put at risk.

Quantity
Infiltration techniques:

- provide storage for runoff. In the case of soakaways and infiltration trenches, this storage is provided in an underground chamber, lined with a porous membrane and filled with coarse crushed rock. Infiltration basins store runoff by temporary and shallow ponding on the surface

- enhance the natural ability of the soil to drain the water. They do this by providing a large surface area in contact with the surrounding soil, through which the water can pass.

The amount of water that can be disposed of by an infiltration device within a specified time depends mainly on the **infiltration potential** of the surrounding soil. The size of the device and the bulk density of any fill material will govern storage capacity.

> **Infiltration potential:** the rate at which water flows through a soil (mm/h). Coarse soils such as sands and gravels have a higher infiltration potential than silts and clays.

Quality

Runoff is treated in a variety of ways in an infiltration device. These include:

⬩ physical filtration to remove solids

⬩ adsorption of particles by the material in the soakaway, trench or surrounding soil

⬩ biochemical reactions with micro-organisms growing on the fill or in the soil.

The level of treatment depends on the size of the media and the length of the flow path through the system, which controls the time it takes the runoff to pass into the surrounding soil. Pre-treatment might be required before polluted runoff is allowed into an infiltration device.

Amenity

Infiltration systems are easy to integrate into a site. They are ideal for use as playing fields, recreational areas or public open space. Infiltration basins can be planted with trees, shrubs and other plants, improving their visual appearance and providing habitats for wildlife. They increase soil moisture content and help to recharge groundwater, thereby mitigating problems of low river flows.

Groundwater protection policy for Scotland (SEPA, 1997) gives advice on the suitability of infiltration devices in particular parts of the country with reference to the impact of surface water on groundwater quality.

Design

Infiltration devices are designed for limited storage and disposal. The volume of storage required is governed by the infiltration potential of the soil, the runoff in the design storm and the time allowed to drain away.

Infiltration devices vary in size from soakaways serving individual houses to basins that collect runoff from entire developments.

Infiltration devices should not be built within 5 m of a building or under a road or on a soil that might dissolve or be washed away. The use of suitable geotextiles can extend the life of the device.

Construction

Heavy vehicles should not be driven over infiltration devices, and they should not be used for storage of materials. Compaction reduces the effectiveness of infiltration devices by making the soil less permeable.

Operation

The device should be inspected at set intervals to ensure it is working correctly. Areas draining to an infiltration device should be kept clear of silt, as this might be washed into the device, reducing the permeability of the soil and filling up space that should be used for storage of runoff.

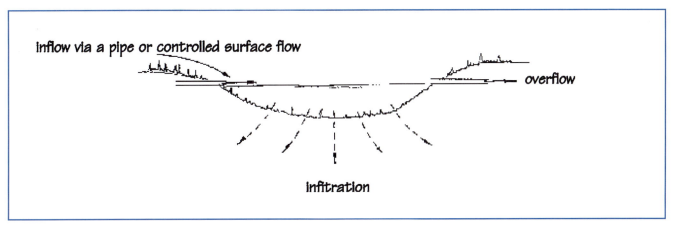

Cross-section through an infiltration basin. The same principles apply for a swale being used for infiltration

Basins and ponds

What are they?

Basins are areas for storage of surface runoff that are free from water under dry weather flow conditions. These structures include:

◆ flood plains

◆ detention basins

◆ extended detention basins.

Ponds contain water in dry weather and are designed to hold more when it rains. They include:

◆ balancing and attenuation ponds

◆ flood storage reservoirs

◆ lagoons

◆ retention ponds

◆ wetlands.

The structures can be mixed, including both a permanently wet area for wildlife or treatment of the runoff and an area that is usually dry to cater for flood attenuation. Basins and ponds tend to be found towards the end of the surface water management train, so are used if source control cannot be fully implemented, if extended treatment of the runoff is required or if they are required for wildlife or landscape reasons.

Basins can be built to fit in with the site plan – even in the middle of roundabouts.
Gravel protected the main flow routes whilst the vegetation became established

Ponds and wetlands can add to a site's ecological value

How they work

Basins and ponds store water at the ground surface, either as temporary flooding of dry basins and flood plains, or in permanent ponds. These structures can be designed to manage water quantity and quality.

Quantity
Basins and ponds can be designed to control flowrates by storing floodwater and releasing it slowly once the risk of flooding has passed (a balancing pond). The stored water will change the water level, and basins and ponds should be designed to function in both dry and wet weather.

Quantity can also be influenced by the amount of water that can infiltrate into the ground if the soil and groundwater conditions are appropriate.

Quality
Basins and ponds treat runoff by:

◆ settlement of solids in still water. Having plants in the water enhances calm conditions and promotes settlement

◆ adsorption of particles by aquatic vegetation or the soil

◆ biological activity.

Amenity
Basins and wetlands offer many opportunities for the landscape designer. Basins should not be built on, but can be

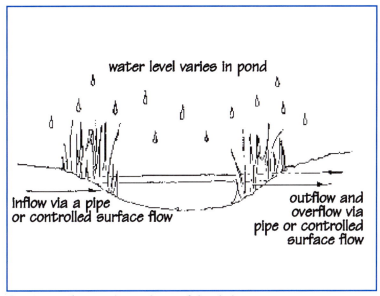

water level varies in pond

inflow via a pipe
or controlled surface flow

outflow and
overflow via
pipe or controlled
surface flow

Ponds may form an integral part of the drainage system and the landscaping

used for sports and recreational areas. Permanently wet ponds can be used to store water for reuse, and offer excellent opportunities for the provision of wildlife habitats and the improvement of the landscape. Both ponds and basins can be part of public open space.

Design

Basins
There are no firm distinctions between the various types of basin, but the following examples show the key design principles:

- natural or constructed flood plains are dry for most of the time, and only store water briefly after severe storms.

- detention basins or balancing ponds provide better flow attenuation. They store water until the flood has passed

- if the period of detention increases to around 24 hours, the basin becomes an extended detention basin. The longer retention time allows more solids to settle out, so these are used for a combination of attenuation and treatment.

  The water level in these types of basin can vary widely and for most of the time the basin could be dry. Any of these basins could be used for infiltration if soil and groundwater conditions are appropriate.

Ponds
Ponds are permanently wet but water depth fluctuates. They can attenuate flows and treat pollutants. They include:

- balancing ponds or flood storage reservoirs that only store runoff until the flood peak has passed and so have little treatment capacity

- lagoons that provide still conditions for settlement of solids, but offer no biological treatment

- retention ponds that have detention periods up to three weeks. They provide a greater degree of treatment than extended detention basins

- wetlands that have permanent water, flowing slowly through the aquatic vegetation. Wetlands have detention periods of up to two weeks and are generally more efficient at treating pollutants than retention ponds.

Ponds and wetlands should be fed by a constant base inflow to avoid drying out. Floods can be routed around ponds to avoid damaging the plant life and creating excessive fluctuation in water levels.

Construction

Construction of basins and ponds is relatively simple. The ground should not be excessively compacted during construction because this reduces infiltration and hampers plant growth.

Vegetation should be fully established before basins and ponds are operational. The use of pot-grown plants and suitably prepared soil can shorten this process. Local varieties of vegetation should be used wherever possible.

Operation

Access will be required to the basins and ponds for inspection, and to allow for the regular cutting of grass, the annual clearance of aquatic vegetation and silt removal as required.

3 Planning SUDS

Drainage in Scotland is split between several authorities with different responsibilities. Recent discussions between these authorities have clarified the maintenance responsibilities for new drainage systems (in most cases) for a trial period. The key to successful decision-making is consultation between developers, professionals and regulatory authorities. This will produce consensus on design criteria and lead to selection of appropriate drainage techniques for each development. Different bodies have these responsibilities in Northern Ireland and different legislation applies, but the need for consultation is the same and the Scottish procedures can be used as a guide.

Responsibilities

Since local government reorganisation in April 1996, surface water drainage responsibilities outside private properties are split between three main bodies:

- local authorities

- water authorities

- the Scottish Environment Protection Agency, SEPA.

Local authorities act as planning authorities, building control authorities and roads authorities. New development, including drainage, requires the approval of local authority planning departments. Roads authorities, water authorities and SEPA are statutory consultees to the planning process. The planning process is therefore used to co-ordinate drainage control for new developments. Local authority-led Flood Appraisal Groups co-ordinate action where catchments include several separate local authorities. NPPG7 (policy guidance on flooding and planning) sets out some of the issues relating to planning and flood management.

Some authorities are committed to SUDS and are working together to promote their use. The use of SUDS now features in some local plans and in planning authorities' policy guidance. Eventually SUDS will be incorporated into local plans. This will reduce the need for early consultation because the regulatory authorities' criteria for drainage design will already have been set out. In the meantime, regulatory authorities are forging agreements and improving the approval process for developers.

Ownership and maintenance

Discussion between authorities has been instrumental in finding solutions to problems caused by drainage constraints.

For example, some local authorities and water authorities have agreements for shared drainage so that a single system can drain water from properties and roads. Under these agreements, shared surface water sewers are owned and maintained by the water authority. The local authority maintains pipes that only serve road drains and empties the gully pots and separators.

The most helpful legislation is Section 7 of the Sewerage (Scotland) Act. This provides for roads and water authorities to enter into agreements for shared drainage and is the basis of the agreement for maintenance of public SUDS.

Water features can be integrated into urban landscapes

COSLA and the Scottish water authorities have drawn up a framework for an agreement to cover the use of SUDS. The working party considers this agreement will facilitate a single agreement between corresponding roads authorities and water authorities for most developments in their area. Under the terms of this framework, maintenance will be shared between water authorities and local authorities, who will maintain below-ground and above-ground facilities respectively. A copy of the framework maintenance agreement is included in Appendix A. Any agreements, including site specific agreements involving third parties, must be competent under current legislation.

1

Ownership and maintenance responsibility for systems that are not covered by shared drainage agreements are as follows:

⬧   owners are responsible for drainage within the curtilage of their properties

⬧   roads authorities are responsible for drainage of adopted roads

⬧   water authorities are responsible for drainage beyond the curtilage of properties (unless the site is served by a private sewer).

Ownership of the land within the curtilage of the property may also change through the development process, with a landowner selling the land to a developer and this then being sold to the final owner. Each party should be aware of any drainage requirements in terms of land use restrictions or maintenance requirements.

Flooding in Belfast, Northern Ireland

Approvals

Formal approval for a drainage system is needed from:

♦ the planning authority (planning permission)

♦ building control authority (building warrant)

♦ the water authority (drainage construction consent)

♦ the roads authority (road construction consent)

♦ SEPA (consent to discharge – if required – or conditional prohibition notice).

Each regulatory authority has its own powers – there is no hierarchy of statutory instruments.

Planning authority
The planning authority draws up structure and local plans. It identifies areas for different land uses in local plans.

The planning system is used to co-ordinate consultation between the approving authorities, but the licence and consents have to be applied for separately – they are not granted automatically when a planning application is approved.

Other interested parties, such as members of the public and non-governmental organisations, also make use of the planning process to promote their views.

Planning authorities can set criteria for the design of the drainage system that will fulfil some of their amenity objectives, such as provision of public open space.

Building control authority
Building control officers have to be satisfied that adequate provision has been made for drainage. The proposed system should be designed and constructed to meet the Technical Standards for compliance with the Building Standards (Scotland) Regulations 1990 (as amended).

Building control departments (building quality departments in some authorities) will therefore be interested in the location of drainage systems and their proximity to structures. Interpretation of the Building Regulations might vary between authorities.

Water authority
In practice, water authorities, as the sewerage authority, issue technical approval of the proposed sewerage infrastructure to serve the development. Provided that the infrastructure is constructed in accordance with the approved layout and in accordance with the water authority's specification it shall generally be accepted.

Roads authority
Construction consent is required from the local authority, as the roads authority, to construct or alter a road that will be adopted by the authority. Connection of a private road or access to the local road network will require the authority's permission. Trunk roads are the responsibility of the Scottish Executive, from whom permission to alter or connect to a trunk road should be sought.

Each authority sets down standards which developers must follow throughout the construction process to ensure that adoptable roads are of satisfactory construction, safe for the public to use and able to be easily maintained. Effective road drainage is fundamentally important to road safety and to the integrity and structural stability of the road, including its footways, verges and margins. When considering construction consent applications local authorities will want to be satisfied that SUDS employed in particular locations meet their road drainage requirements and will not require onerous maintenance.

SEPA

The Control of Pollution Act 1974 (as amended) gives SEPA powers to consent discharges to **controlled waters**. The Act defines three categories of discharge:

- trade effluent

- sewage effluent

- matter other than trade or sewage effluent. Surface water discharges are regarded as "other matter".

Discharges of "other matter" to controlled waters do not require consent unless SEPA serves a prohibition notice. Such a notice may be absolute (requiring a discharger to apply for consent) or conditional. Discharges of "other matter" to land are not subject to SEPA's statutory control.

Controlled waters: Controlled waters are defined by the Control of Pollution Act 1974 (as amended). Generally, controlled waters include:

- relevant territorial waters for 3 miles seaward from the shore

- coastal waters

- inland waters above the freshwater limit (including relevant lochs, ponds, reservoirs and canals)

- groundwaters.

It is SEPA's intention not to place numeric quality standards on consents or conditional prohibition notices, provided that surface water drainage systems are designed in accordance with this manual. SEPA intends to regulate discharges from sustainable urban drainage systems by conditional prohibition notices, requiring drainage to be installed in accordance with the design, ie use of descriptive conditions. Only in exceptional circumstances would an absolute prohibition notice be used to control discharges from SUDS by a consent, for example large developments discharging to sensitive waters.

2

Even if a consent to discharge is unlikely to be required, the procedures in this manual should be followed to make sure SEPA is aware of the drainage proposals.

The approval process

Consultation with the regulatory authorities is essential because their responsibilities and interests overlap. For example, local authorities are responsible for the prevention and control of flooding within their boundaries, while SEPA has a legal duty to provide flood risk advice to planning authorities based on information held. Consensus needs to be reached between the authorities so that the developer does not receive contradictory advice.

3

Initial consultation

The purpose of this early consultation is:

- to make all interested parties aware that development is proposed

- to identify constraints and criteria for the drainage design.

The developer should contact the planning authority as early as possible to discuss proposed schemes. This pre-application stage might be when a landowner is considering selling property or when a developer is considering purchasing a site for development.

After the developer has contacted the planning authority, the planners may convene a meeting if it is considered appropriate. This should be decided in consultation with interested stakeholders such as SEPA or the water authority. The developer should submit an **outline development concept** to enable the planners to decide on the meeting's scope and to brief the participants beforehand if necessary. For large developments the meeting might just cover surface water drainage whereas for small projects the meeting might cover all planning issues. The statutory authorities need to attend the meeting ready to advise the developer on the design criteria for water quantity, quality and amenity issues appropriate to the site. The authorities will need to be aware of impacts that might occur outwith the site and so might need to consult with organisations with interests upstream or downstream of the development.

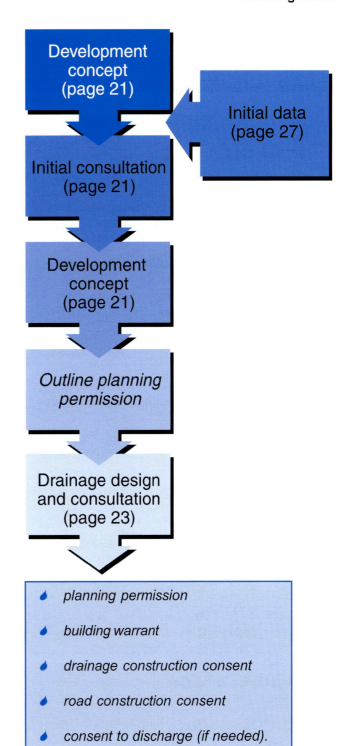

- planning permission

- building warrant

- drainage construction consent

- road construction consent

- consent to discharge (if needed).

Outline development concept: the developer should submit a location plan and a brief sketch describing the development concept.

The meeting should be attended by some or all of the following:

- the local authority planner

- the developer and the drainage designers

- a SEPA area representative

- a water authority representative

- a building control representative

- a roads authority representative

- other local authority representatives as appropriate.

The meeting should have the following outcomes:

- the authorities should be aware of the proposed scale and type of development

- the developer should have qualitative guidance from the authorities on the basic surface water drainage design criteria (quantity, quality and amenity); these are discussed in Chapter 4 of this manual

- information should be exchanged on any known special features of the site

- lines of communication for further consultation should be clear

- the authorities should decide if more detailed proposals on the drainage system need to be submitted in advance of a planning application. This should not be necessary for small or straightforward developments.

As with any development, the designers should also contact the various utility companies (including sewerage undertakers) and bodies such as RoSPA and SNH (Scottish Natural Heritage). Consultation should cover both design, construction and operational issues.

Outline drainage proposals
Initial consultation should provide enough information for a drainage proposal to be drawn up using the decision tool described in Chapter 4. If the planners require information in advance of the full planning application, a drainage proposal should be submitted, indicating which of the following measures are to be used:

- prevention

- source control

- conveyance

- site control

- regional control.

The proposal should state which drainage techniques will be considered in the detailed design and describe ideas for integrating the drainage system into the landscape or required public open space. At this stage there is no need to submit initial calculations, but they should be carried out to roughly size any significant drainage structures. This will allow the percentage land take of different options to be estimated.

Depending on the outcome of the initial consultation and the **scale** and complexity of the proposed development, further informal liaison with regulatory authorities might be required when drawing up the drainage strategy.

The strategy should be submitted as part of the outline planning application.

> **Scale:** large developments can be drained in exactly the same way as single houses, using source control. However, the planning processes may differ, with major schemes requiring master plans drawn up to guide each stage. Small proposals could have a much simpler route through the approval process.

Water features can be an integral part of public open space

Drainage design and consultation

This stage involves preparation of a detailed drainage design for submission with the full planning application and the applications for other approvals. Five steps are needed.

1. The planning authority should agree with the other regulatory authorities on the type of information that needs to be included in the planning application. Appendix B of this manual gives an example of the information required. The planning authority should inform the developer of the requirements.

2. The developer and drainage designer should liaise as necessary with the regulatory authorities to agree on appropriate criteria.

3. The drainage designer should follow the procedures in this manual for selection of drainage techniques.

4. The developer should confirm with the regulatory authorities that the selected techniques are appropriate.

5. The drainage designer should follow the guidance in this manual to produce designs for the planning, building warrant, drainage and road construction applications.

Further meetings between the developers and the authorities will be required only if there is a need for further discussion about design criteria or techniques, or if the development is very large and complex.

Throughout this process the planning authority should act as co-ordinator and maintain contact with SEPA, the water authority and other local authority functions.

At the end of this stage, the information needed by all the regulatory authorities will have been assembled. Although separate applications will be made to each regulatory authority the drainage proposals should be approved by all of them.

Even formal ponds can cater for wildlife. Here a ramp has been provided for waterfowl.

Designers

As the drainage design has to take into account a wider variety of considerations than conventional drainage schemes, a team approach will help integrate the various expert inputs required. The design team should include:

◆ hydrologists. The assessment of runoff from greenfield sites and forecasting the response from a developed site is a specialist task. Various computer programs are available to help with this process, but knowledge and experience are needed to ensure that the results are meaningful. SUDS require several scenarios to be examined, rather than just a single **design storm**.

◆ landscape architects and ecologists. SUDS make use of vegetation to treat flows and prevent erosion. Integrating the drainage system with the surrounding land use will also require the designer to select appropriate hard (paving) or soft (**planting**) landscape features.

◆ engineers. Even though many SUDS devices make use of landscape features such as earthworks, these need to be designed to ensure stability. Other areas where engineering expertise is required are hydraulic design of channels, basins and wetlands, together with the associated inlets, outlets and overflows, the structural engineering of pavements and the hydrogeology of infiltration devices.

> **Design storm:** Simple pipe systems are often designed to cope with a "design storm" that has a specified intensity and duration. This does not take into account the runoff from bigger storms or the flow pattern from minor events.
>
> SUDS require the assessment of a variety of runoff events to ensure a wider range of design considerations is met.

> **Planting:** Appropriate plants need to be selected for some SUDS. Design considerations include:
>
> ◆ the surrounding land use
> ◆ the bio-engineering requirements
> ◆ growth patterns
> ◆ the maintenance regime
> ◆ any biodiversity or wildlife requirements
> ◆ the climate, water regime and soil type.
>
> Native plants are to be preferred where possible, but these do need to be carefully selected to ensure adequate growth and local suitability.

Legislation

Legislation affecting drainage is complex.
Sustainable urban drainage techniques were not
practised in Scotland when the legislation was
passed, so are not dealt with explicitly.

Sewerage Authorities have a duty under Section 1 (1) of the Sewerage (Scotland) Act 1968 (as amended by the Local Government etc. (Scotland) Act 1994) "to provide such public sewers as may be necessary for effectually draining their area of domestic sewage, surface water and trade effluent . . .", and to deal with the contents of their sewers, by treatment or otherwise.

Section 1 (2) (a) of the Act requires the sewerage authority, subject to paragraph (b) " to take their public sewers to such point or points as will enable the owners of premises which are to be served by the sewers to connect their drains or private sewers with the public sewers at reasonable cost."

Section 1 (2) (b) states "where the sewerage authority have agreed with some other person (in this Section referred to as the "private provider") that he will take a private sewer to such point or points as will enable owners to make such connection as is mentioned in paragraph (a) above, that paragraph shall not apply while the agreement subsists".

Section 1 (3) states "The duties imposed by the foregoing subsections shall not require a sewerage authority to do anything which is not practicable at a reasonable cost."

Section 1 (4) gives recourse to the Secretary of State if a dispute arises regarding the question of practicability at a reasonable cost, or the point to which sewers must be taken.

Section 8 (1) allows the sewerage authority to enter into an agreement as to provision of sewers etc for new premises.

Section 8 (2) states that "An agreement under the foregoing section may only be entered into by an authority where the authority have no duty under Section 1 above to provide public sewers to serve the premises."

To summarise, the sewerage authority have a duty to drain a development of domestic sewage, surface water (defined by the Act as "the runoff of rainwater from roofs and any paved ground surface within the curtilage of premises") and trade effluent, provided it is practicable at a reasonable cost.

If it is deemed not to be practicable at a reasonable cost then no duty exists, but the developer may seek to enter into an agreement under Section 8 of the Act.

4 Selecting SUDS

Sustainable urban drainage systems are designed using the same underlying principles of hydrology and hydraulics as conventional drainage systems, but applying them in a different way. Alongside the purely technical issues are wider considerations of amenity and integration with the environment. The selection process outlined below is designed to generate a range of possible solutions, from which a system that satisfies all parties can be chosen. The design process is iterative, with the designers reviewing options to meet the combined needs of water quality, flood risk and amenity.

Principles

When selecting SUDS it is important to consider quality, quantity and amenity **design criteria** equally. There will not be a single "correct" answer: several options may meet the design criteria, and judgement will be needed. This is illustrated by the example later in this manual.

> **Design criteria:** a set of conditions agreed by the developer, planners and regulators that the proposed system should satisfy.

Selection and design of SUDS are multi-disciplinary processes. Unlike conventional drainage systems, factors that influence the final choice will include landscape, architectural and planning requirements.

Before the drainage system is selected and designed, data is needed on the site and the planned development.

Initial data needs

The developer will need to collect certain information for the planning process. This will be needed to:

- find out what the existing conditions are

- state the concepts of the proposed development

- allow the impact of the proposals to be assessed.

This will enable the design criteria to be developed. More detailed information will be required for the next iteration of the design process. A checklist is provided in Appendix B.

Original drainage pattern

The natural drainage pattern of the site is a good starting point for the drainage system. One of the main design criteria for water quantity management should be to minimise changes to the flow regime of the local area. There are exceptions. If an industrial site is built on permeable soils that would normally allow free infiltration, pollution in the runoff might contaminate the groundwater. In such cases runoff might have to be treated to remove pollutants before infiltration could be considered.

Example of natural drainage inspiring a constructed system

Catchment topography

An assessment of the topography of the area needs to be made. This will influence the choice of drainage methods and provide basic information to calculate the runoff of the existing catchments.

Local rainfall and runoff

To establish the runoff of the site before and after development, rainfall data and information on the current land use will be required, just as for conventional drainage design.

Locations of discharges

Designers should determine the location of the discharges from the drainage system. This may be to a surface water body (either directly or via surface water sewer), to a combined sewer or to land. The location may influence selection decisions for SUDS and needs to be considered at an early stage. Ideally, surface runoff should be returned to the environment in as many locations as possible, spreading the impact on receiving waters. The location of the discharge will have implications for water quality and quantity.

Ground conditions

If infiltration is to be considered as a drainage option, an initial assessment of the soil characteristics will need to be made. The best way to do this is by site infiltration tests, as described in BRE Digest 365, Soakaway design, and CIRIA Report 156, Infiltration drainage – manual of good practice.

A general indication of whether the area is suitable for infiltration can be obtained by reference to SEPA's Groundwater protection policy for Scotland, 1997, and the **WRAP** or **HOST** classifications from maps contained in the *Flood studies report (1975)* and *Flood estimation handbook (1999)*, both published by the Institute of Hydrology.

The development

The developer will need to give information on the proposed development. One item of primary importance to the management of runoff quality will be the proposed pattern of land use. In particular it will be useful to know if potentially polluting activities are grouped together or scattered throughout the development.

Discrete drainage areas should be identified, to enable local management of the runoff. These should be as small as is reasonable. The planned topography and land use will determine the sub-catchments and the resulting runoff response.

Other

The design will take into account issues that are not normally associated with drainage design, so the site should be examined for existing wildlife habitats, landscape features and community uses.

> **WRAP** (Winter Rain Acceptance Potential) and **HOST** (Hydrology Of Soil Types) are classifications that are used to indicate the permeability of the soil and the percentage runoff from a particular area. The lower the percentage runoff, the more suitable the soil is for infiltration.

The quality and use of the receiving water is important in drainage design

Establishing design criteria

In the initial discussions about the drainage system, strategies will need to be evaluated to establish design criteria. These will have to include agreed processes for the management of quantity and quality as well as indicating any amenity issues that should be addressed.

Some **design considerations** are discussed later in this section. The design itself will be site-specific, so it will be necessary to view these design considerations in the light of the local conditions.

The regulatory authorities should identify design criteria at the outset of the planning process, based on the concepts set out by the developer, the information on the site and the regulators' planning, management and environmental considerations. A sample checklist is included as Appendix B.

> **Design considerations** are discussed during the planning process to develop site-specific **design criteria**.

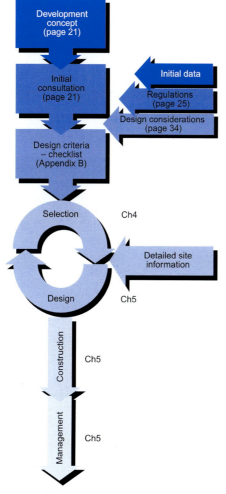

Using the selection tool

Once an initial assessment of the site has been made and the design strategies for the drainage system have been agreed, drainage techniques can be selected.

The selection tool that follows is based on the surface water management train introduced earlier. It is designed to lead the designers through the selection process, in accordance with the principles that:

- ♦ drainage techniques will be used in series to meet the design criteria

- ♦ drainage techniques at the top of the management train are generally to be preferred to those further downstream

- ♦ there is no single correct solution – selection may be the result of factors outwith the normal remit of drainage designers

- ♦ the drainage system should be inspired by the original drainage pattern.

4

The process is cyclical, and various factors have to be considered in increasing detail as a final solution is approached. Some of the additional factors that may influence the choice are discussed later in this section.

The suggested route to select a drainage system is not rigorous; value judgements have to be given and subjective assessments made of the capabilities of the site.

Do not approach the selection process as a linear path through the flowchart – the decisions required should be put in a wider context than just the pure technical details.

Selection tool

There are many issues that have to be considered in selecting a sustainable urban drainage system. The number of potential solutions is also extensive, especially when all the different combinations are taken into consideration. The design of drainage systems should be a team exercise and the following route is suggested to structure the decision-making process.

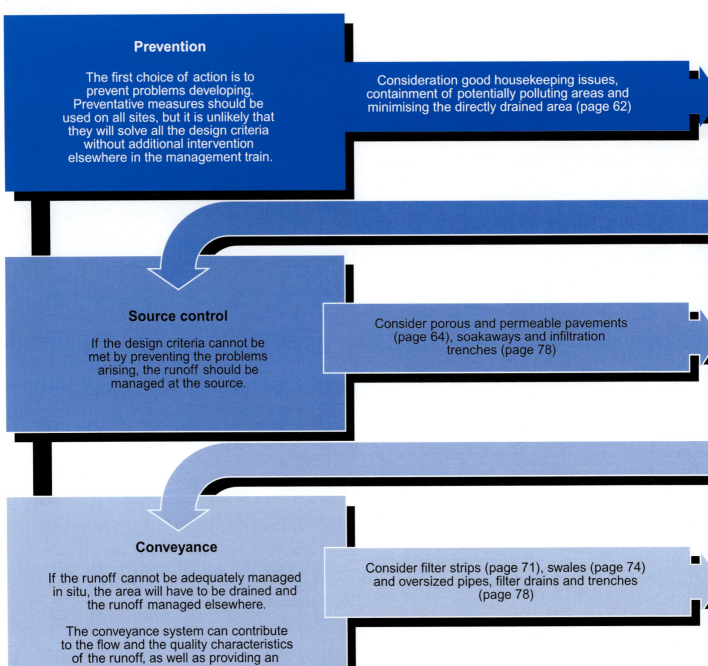

Prevention

The first choice of action is to prevent problems developing. Preventative measures should be used on all sites, but it is unlikely that they will solve all the design criteria without additional intervention elsewhere in the management train.

Consideration good housekeeping issues, containment of potentially polluting areas and minimising the directly drained area (page 62)

Source control

If the design criteria cannot be met by preventing the problems arising, the runoff should be managed at the source.

Consider porous and permeable pavements (page 64), soakaways and infiltration trenches (page 78)

Conveyance

If the runoff cannot be adequately managed in situ, the area will have to be drained and the runoff managed elsewhere.

The conveyance system can contribute to the flow and the quality characteristics of the runoff, as well as providing an opportunity to enhance the environment.

Consider filter strips (page 71), swales (page 74) and oversized pipes, filter drains and trenches (page 78)

It should be borne in mind however that this framework is not a mechanistic process: value judgements and choices will have to be made between disparate objectives. The design will be iterative, with a short assessment of the options at the planning stage followed by more detailed analysis as the design proceeds.

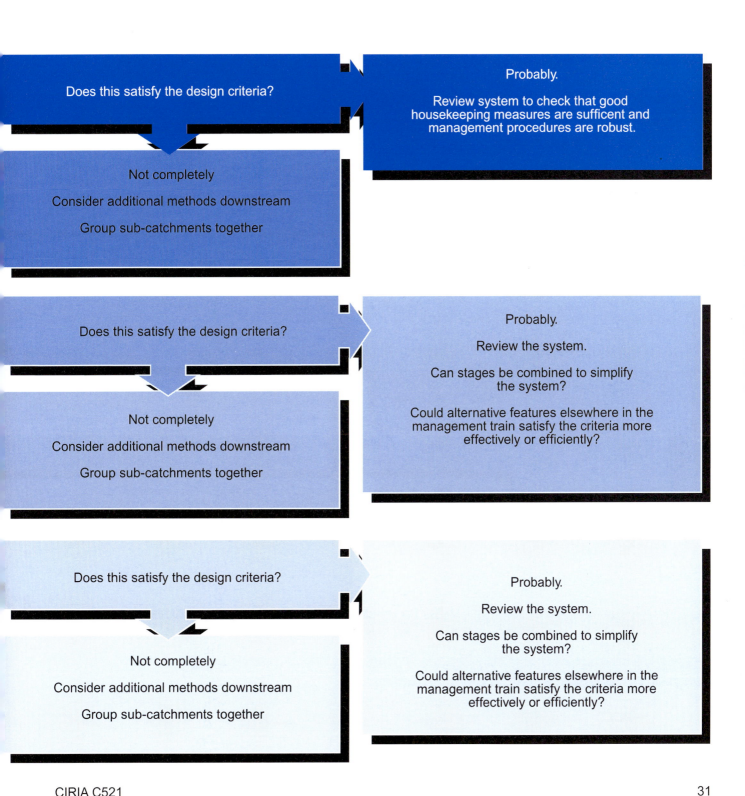

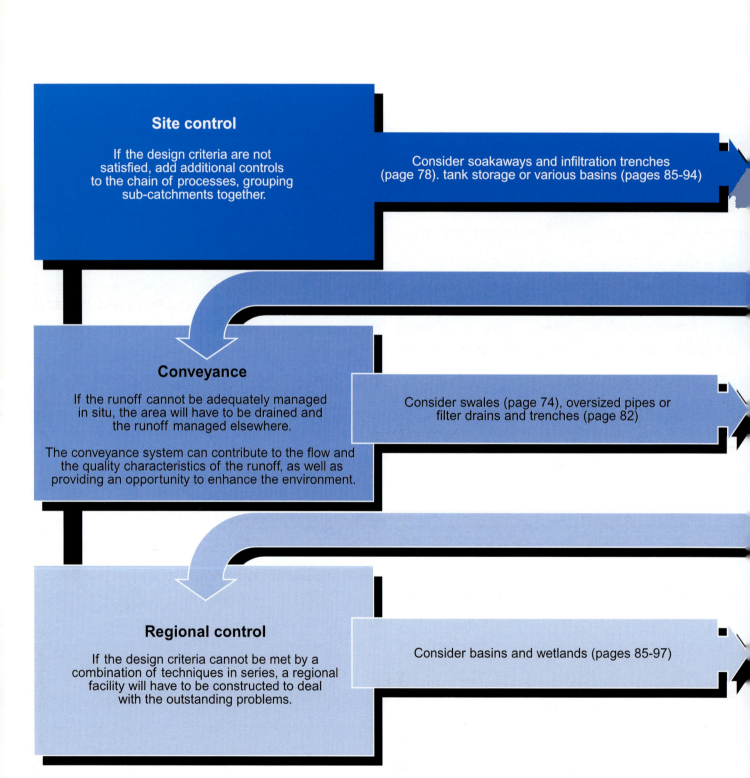

Site control

If the design criteria are not
satisfied, add additional controls
to the chain of processes, grouping
sub-catchments together.

Consider soakaways and infiltration trenches
(page 78). tank storage or various basins (pages 85-94)

Conveyance

If the runoff cannot be adequately managed
in situ, the area will have to be drained and
the runoff managed elsewhere.

The conveyance system can contribute to the flow and
the quality characteristics of the runoff, as well as
providing an opportunity to enhance the environment.

Consider swales (page 74), oversized pipes or
filter drains and trenches (page 82)

Regional control

If the design criteria cannot be met by a
combination of techniques in series, a regional
facility will have to be constructed to deal
with the outstanding problems.

Consider basins and wetlands (pages 85-97)

Judging whether the design criteria have been satisfied will involve a mixture of objective and subjective analyses. Experience and good judgement will be of the utmost importance. Even technical considerations such as flood risk will need to be judged on the reliability of the forecasts and the relevance of the data.

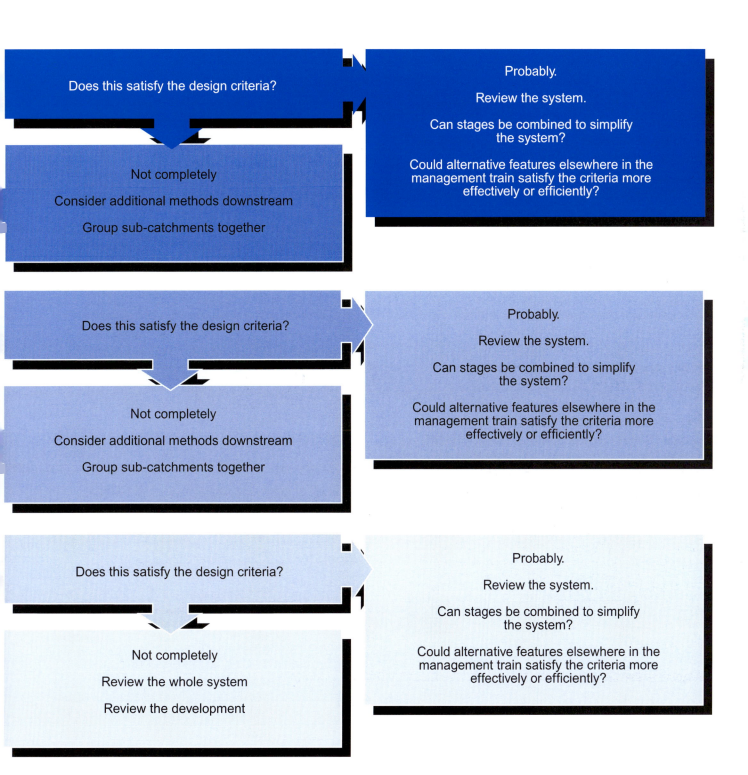

Design considerations

These design considerations are indicative only. All parties will need to agree design criteria for each site at the start of the planning process, using these suggestions as a starting-point for the discussions. Criteria might have to be more onerous or be relaxed, depending on site factors. It might be necessary to use several SUDS in series to control the quantity and quality of the runoff, or satisfy the agreed amenity criteria. Parallel flow routes might be needed to divert high flows.

General runoff considerations

Many of the problems with conventional drainage result from the separation of different objectives. For clarity, the various design considerations are discussed under the headings of quantity, quality and amenity, but the balance illustrated by the urban drainage triangle on page 2 should be maintained.

As an example, flows will need to be examined for a series of **flood frequencies**. Organisations responsible for flood management may need forecasts of the water levels resulting from various flows to assess the areas at risk. A local authority might require information on the floods with frequencies of 20, 10, 3.3, 2 and 0.83 per cent. Insurance companies might need to know the level of the 0.5 per cent frequency flood. However, water quality considerations depend on smaller, more frequent runoff events, with **recurrence intervals** of less than two years. Amenity issues will require a similar range of analysis, to see how often public open space may flood, and for how long. The baseflows will be important, to ensure watercourses and ponds do not dry out in periods of extended dry weather and impact on wildlife and plants.

5

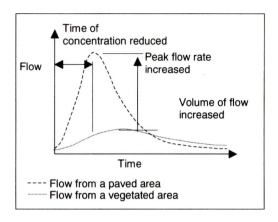

Hydrograph showing the impact of development on the flow regime

Quantity considerations

One of the basic aims of a sustainable drainage system is to drain the site without adversely affecting the river regime downstream. It is evident that increasing the amount of paved area leads to an increase in the peak flow and volume of runoff, and reduces the time of concentration.

Ideally the runoff hydrograph should be similar before and after development. As a starting-point for discussion it is suggested that the peak flow, the time of concentration and the baseflow resulting from the developed site should be broadly similar to those from the undeveloped site. Thus the runoff from a developed site resulting from a particular storm should have the same peak flow occurring at a similar time to the runoff that would have resulted if the site was still undeveloped.

6

The level of accuracy available in estimating these figures should always be taken into account when the flow regime is discussed.

Flood frequencies: Flowrates that are exceeded on average once every 50 years have a probability of 2 per cent that they would be exceeded in a single year.

Recurrence intervals are used to define smaller flows that would be exceeded more frequently than say once every five years.

Organisations might require assessments of the flow at different locations. These might include a flood-prone area downstream or a drainage feature that could cause water to back up and create flooding upstream. An appraisal of the impact of the development on the watercourse at these points could be required. Where the drainage pattern is being changed at several points in a catchment, the cumulative effect might have to be assessed. Designers should be aware that drainage extends upstream as well as downstream. Flooding can be caused by flows backing up the drainage system. The interaction between various parts of the surface water management train will have to be considered, including any conventional piped drainage in the system.

7

Onstream: dry weather flow passes through the storage area.

Offstream: dry weather flow bypasses the storage area.

The **flow route** that the runoff takes will have to be considered for each flood frequency under consideration. Overflows or spillways might need to be built for **onstream** drainage features to ensure that no excessive damage is caused by the high flowrates. Severe but infrequent floods will be important for large catchments, whereas more frequent floods affect small sub-catchments. The runoff from these more frequent storms should be drained quickly from roads and footways to avoid ponding on the surface. Ponding due to runoff should be managed to ensure it does not regularly inconvenience people.

8

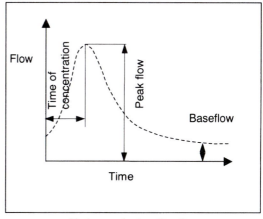

*Hydrograph showing the
main design parameters to be considered*

Sample considerations for **water levels**. This is an example only and the balance between the costs of managing each different flow rate will have to be balanced with the benefits that would be achieved. This has to be done on a site by site basis in order to avoid excessive expenditure for limited benefits.

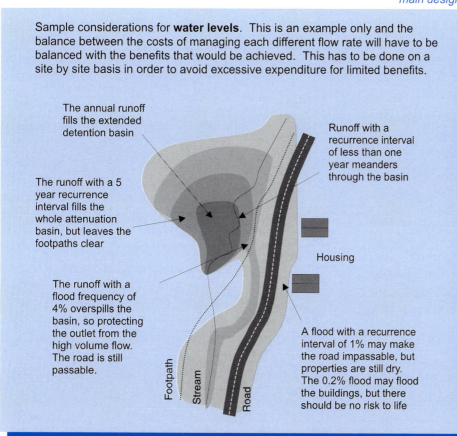

Areas that flood frequently should not cause adverse impacts

Flow routes: Runoff from small storms and the start of large storms may contain pollutants. These flows should be routed through the drainage system to treat the pollutants.

Runoff from large storms may inundate or damage parts of the drainage system, such as wetlands, so less frequent events that cannot be sufficiently attenuated should be routed to limit their adverse impact.

Low flows should also be calculated, and landscaping designed so that watercourses and basins do not look out of place in dry weather.

The baseflow will not be an issue at all sites, but if there are problems due to low flows in local watercourses, the design criteria might include a requirement for infiltration to replenish groundwater, even if this means reducing the volume of surface flow from the site.

Water quantity estimation

Water quantity estimation is an inexact science. All parties involved should be aware of the difficulties in predicting the rainfall/runoff characteristics of a catchment before and after development. A common sense approach has to be taken, especially where local data is sparse.

Runoff estimation

The *Flood estimation handbook*, which replaces the *Flood studies report (Institute of Hydrology)* provides guidance on the estimation of flood flows. It should be stressed however that there will always be some uncertainty over any modelled runoff response. This is because of the number of factors that influence the runoff response and the variation within each of the factors. Accurate predictions can only be attempted with extensive local data, which is rarely available.

Flood estimation normally considers whole river catchments so caution should be used when extrapolating estimates to small areas. This is especially true of flows with long return periods.

Some characteristics of urban catchments are:

- increased runoff from reduced-permeability surfaces (especially true if the soils are naturally permeable)

- decreased baseflow because of reduced permeability

- conventional piped drainage reduces the time to peak flow, making the catchment more sensitive to short-duration storms

- changes in critical seasons – rural catchments tend to flood after long winter storms while urban sites tend to be more at risk from short, heavy summer storms

- variation in physical characteristics (such as permeability) between sub-catchments

- sub-catchments have different response times to rainfall because they have different characteristics. Catchment interaction can either mitigate flooding or increase it.

The procedure to estimate the catchment response should be discussed at the outline planning stage to ensure that an agreed method is used. Modelling the catchment has to be carried out with a sense of perspective. Various computer packages are available, but intricate computer simulations are not always the best course of action. Simpler models may be all that the available data warrants.

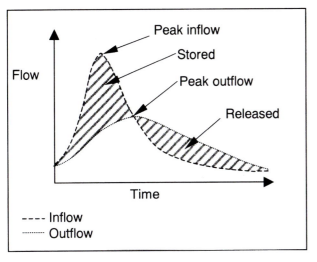

Hydrograph showing the impact of attenuation through a pond

Examples of possible flow estimation methods include:

♦ the Modified Rational Method (*Wallingford Procedure*, HR Wallingford, 1981)

♦ the Unit Hydrograph Method (Institute of Hydrology, 1985)

♦ the Simplified Flood Estimation Method detailed in *Design of flood storage reservoirs* (CIRIA, 1993).

Advice and data should be available from the water and local authorities with support from SEPA.

Attenuation

High runoff rates can be reduced by attenuating the flows. This can be carried out in two ways:

♦ reservoir routing uses online or offline storage to hold back excess volume, which is released once the flow peak has passed. A large plan area and small change in depth will provide more attenuation than a small area and a large variation in depth

♦ attenuation also occurs along a filter drain, swale or watercourse. If no additional flow is added to a river or pipe, the peak flow rate will diminish as it travels along a reach. Attenuation in a channel can be enhanced by using shallow gradients, large wetted perimeters and high roughness coefficients.

Other methods of attenuating flows include using tanks and oversized pipes for storage with the flow controlled by downstream throttles, orifices, hydraulic controls or actuated valves. The cumulative effect of attenuation devices in series should be calculated.

Hydraulics

The hydraulic design of sustainable drainage structures will be subject to a greater level of uncertainty than design using a piped system. This is because natural variability will play an important role in determining channel parameters such as roughness and cross-section. Calculations are subject to individual judgement, and some sensitivity analysis may be necessary for critical structures.

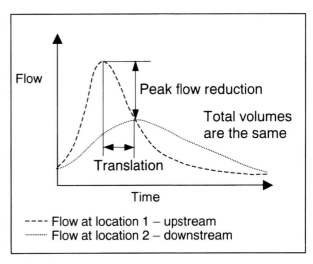

Hydrograph showing the impact of attenuation along a river reach

Infiltration

Infiltration should be used wherever possible to continue the natural drainage pattern. However, many soils in Scotland and Northern Ireland are fairly impermeable (such as clays and boulder clays), so infiltration techniques might not be suitable. It is recommended that infiltration tests are carried out on all sites where this method of disposal is being considered.

Even where soils are relatively impermeable, water can still soak into the soil using the natural storage capacity and drain horizontally (interflow) to a nearby watercourse or swale. Management of the rainfall at the point where it hits the ground is the ideal source control and should be used where possible.

Construction activity may compact soils and reduce the infiltration potential.

On very permeable soil, features such as wetlands may require impermeable liners to prevent the area draining unintentionally. Even if the soil is permeable, a high water table may prevent the use of infiltration features.

Example of a hydraulic control structure

Runoff disposed of by infiltration replenishes the groundwater resource. This is usually a benefit, but if the groundwater is sensitive to pollution, the runoff might have to be treated before it is allowed to infiltrate. This might also be the case in very permeable soils, where pollutants are not kept within the soil long enough to be treated. In some cases infiltration will be prohibited. Guidance can be found in SEPA's *Groundwater protection policy for Scotland* (SEPA, 1997).

Quality considerations

Surface water runoff can wash pollutants into watercourses or the soil. The nature and the amount of pollution is difficult to quantify and highly dependent upon the land use within the catchment. For instance a yard area where chemicals are handled is more at risk of pollution than a driveway to a residential property. The impact of surface water runoff is difficult to predict and is dependent upon the nature and sensitivity of the receiving waters. In addition, the effects of urban drainage are cumulative over time as a catchment becomes urbanised. Therefore designers and regulators need to consider the long-term effects of discharges.

Treatment stage: a single drainage device adequately sized for the volume of runoff judged to be potentially polluted (treatment volume).

Sensitivity of environments:
Designers need to be aware that some receiving waters are particularly sensitive. In such instances SUDS might need to be designed with additional treatment capacity in order to protect the environment. This may be achieved by passing surface water runoff through additional stages in the surface water management train.

Examples of particularly sensitive receiving environments include:

- bathing areas
- receiving waters that pass through formal public parks/picnic sites/formal open spaces
- designated shellfish waters
- designated freshwater fish waters
- sites with a statutory ecological designation, eg sites of special scientific interest containing habitats or species worthy of protection
- undesignated sites that have features deemed worthy of protection.

SUDS might not be required for water quality purposes for less sensitive waters – for example small developments that discharge to high-dilution waterbodies such as estuaries or coastal waters not considered sensitive.

Device	Residential	Non-residential	Industrial
Prevention	*	*	*
Containment	–	–	1
Permeable surfaces	1	1	1 (contained)
Filter strips/treatment swales	1	1	2
Filter drains/pavement sub-base	1	1 or 2	2 (contained)
Swales	1	1 or 2	2
Extended detention basins	1	2	2
Soakaways/infiltration trenches	1	2	3
Infiltration basins	1	2	3
Retention ponds	1	2	3
Wetlands	1	2	3
Levels of treatment required	**1**	**2**	**3**

Key

*	–	always required
1	–	first level of treatment
2	–	second level of treatment
3	–	third level of treatment

For a particular land use, the number and order of treatment stages are shown, with alternative drainage methods shown for each level. For example, an industrial site requires three levels of treatment. The first level can be achieved using a lined porous or permeable pavement, with a filter strip or swale providing the second level, followed by a wetland or retention basin to give the third level of treatment.
For trunk roads, see the text.
All sites should have preventative (good housekeeping) measures.

Summary of design strategies for water quality

Each discharge from a drainage system will need to be considered in terms of:

● the risk of pollution

● the **sensitivity** of the receiving water environment.

These factors need to be considered when deciding the level of treatment that a drainage system should provide. It is likely that some level of treatment will be required for all surface water drainage.

A suggested approach to setting the level of treatment is to define the number of stages of the management train that the runoff will pass through before it is discharged to the environment. This can be based on land use. Runoff from sites with a low risk of pollution may be discharged after a single **treatment stage**,

whereas runoff from an area with a higher risk of pollution should pass through a series of devices to ensure a reasonable level of treatment. The considerations below should be used as the basis for discussion between designers and regulators about individual sites.

> All developments should incorporate good housekeeping measures to minimise the potential for pollution. Careful consideration of the site layout might provide opportunities to minimise potentially polluted areas.

9

Management measures such as these are unlikely to ensure reasonable water quality protection by themselves, so structural devices will need to be provided.

Selecting SUDS

Ideally, runoff from non-polluting areas will be routed around the treatment systems, but if the catchment includes both permeable and impermeable areas, the devices should be sized to cater for runoff from both areas.

Residential sites
Unless the receiving water requires a high level of protection, a single treatment stage is likely to be sufficient for residential areas. This could occur anywhere in the management train, but preference should be given to source control methods.

10

Runoff from residential areas needs to pass through only one stage of treatment

Non-residential sites
Non-residential sites include light commercial areas, shops, schools and offices. Some small areas within these sites such as fuel tanks or rubbish skips should be treated as industrial sub-catchments.

Good housekeeping measures are more likely to be effective if the site is owned and maintained by a single body. Even so, preventative measures alone are unlikely to provide an acceptable level of protection, so additional stages of treatment will be needed.

Unless the receiving water is particularly sensitive, two levels of treatment will typically be required. This might consist of source control followed by a site or regional control.

11

Industrial and major commercial sites
Industrial areas pose a greater threat to the environment than other land uses. Extra stages of runoff treatment are therefore required, especially for sensitive receiving waters.

Good housekeeping measures are essential. Using containment systems such as bunds will allow any spills to be controlled in high-risk areas. Covering areas such as garage forecourts will allow rainfall to be directed to the drainage system without being polluted. The area subject to spills can be drained separately without having to cater for the extra volume from rainfall runoff. For further details see *Design of containment systems for the prevention of water pollution from industrial incidents (CIRIA, 1997)*.

12

The following areas could be connected to the foul sewer, subject to the agreement of the water authority:

- permanent skip areas

- yard areas where chemicals and oils might be spilled

- delivery bays where there is a risk of spillage

- designated pressure washing areas

- fuelling areas covered by SEPA PPG3, *The use and design of oil separators in surface water drainage systems.*

These areas should be clearly defined and kept to a minimum to limit the volume of water discharged to the foul sewer. Discharges of trade effluent must be in accordance with consents issued under the Sewerage (Scotland) Act or the Control of Pollution Act.

Vegetated devices need time to get established

Swales are favoured for conveyance because they allow spillages and wrong connections to be identified. Misconnections cannot be made, as there will be no surface water sewer to connect to. Where infiltration is suitable there should be some method of monitoring the flow quality and rapidly identifying problems so intervention can occur before the water leaves the drainage system.

Even if potentially polluting areas are contained, the risk of pollution is still relatively high, so the drainage from the whole industrial site should pass through three treatment stages.

Once vegetation is established it needs to be maintained

Roads

Traffic accidents represent the highest risks to the environment from roads. The Scottish Executive will decide case by case on the need for containment systems for trunk roads. These design considerations apply to operational runoff.

The design criteria for roads, set out at the outline planning stage, will depend on:

◆ the sensitivity of the receiving water

◆ the traffic conditions (traffic flows and the types of vehicle).

If the receiving water is not particularly sensitive to pollution and the road does not have a high traffic flow, the quality criteria are similar to those for a residential site. Where these factors become more significant, a specific assessment – as described in the *Design Manual for Roads and Bridges* (The Stationery Office) – might be necessary to determine the requirements for treatment.

Permeable paving systems should not be proposed for trunk roads and will probably not be suitable for adoptable roads in Scotland. This is because of concerns over structural strength and ground stability.

13

Construction sites

During construction of a development additional drainage measures may be required. These should be discussed with the regulatory authorities site by site (see *Prevention of pollution from construction sites*, CIRIA, 2000).

Temporary pre-treatment may be needed before the runoff enters the drainage system. If infiltration measures or permeable surfaces are to form part of the final drainage system, these will have to be protected from the large quantities of silt that arise during construction.

If vegetated areas are to be used, such as swales, these will also have to be protected from erosion until the plants have time to establish.

14

Brownfield sites

On uncontaminated brownfield sites, the water quality design criteria will depend on the existing sewerage infrastructure. If the water is discharged to a separate surface water sewer or directly to a watercourse, the site should be treated as an undeveloped site and the quality criteria will relate to the proposed land use as set out above.

If the site drains to a combined sewer that is unlikely to be converted to a separate system, the surface water should be treated with a single stage of treatment to remove grit and coarse solids. Foul sewage should be drained separately within the site. Industrial sites might also require containment or special conditions subject to the trade effluent consent.

An important *quality* criterion for all sites draining to combined sewers is the *quantity* of runoff. Storm flows trigger combined sewer overflows, causing foul pollution. They can also overload wastewater treatment works, reducing treatment efficiencies. The flow should be attenuated to match undeveloped rates. In exceptional cases the water authority might request that the runoff is detained completely and only released at night.

15

Contaminated land

Where a contaminated site is proposed for redevelopment, SUDS may be used for the surface water drainage. However, the design of the drainage system will be site-specific and dependent upon the contaminants at the site, the remediation strategy and the risks posed by any residual contamination, in addition to the normal design considerations.

The developer will need to consult with the planning authority and demonstrate that the proposed drainage system should not cause remobilisation of contaminants resulting in exposure to the wider environment. For instance, ground conditions might be suitable for infiltration, but the drainage system could be designed to keep the surface environment separate from the residual contamination below ground. Remediation and redevelopment of contaminated land is a complex subject that requires specialist knowledge (see CIRIA series *Remedial treatment for contaminated land,* SP101-SP112, for further information).

16

Water quality estimation

The quality of runoff is not explicitly considered in conventional drainage design. In a more sustainable system the aim should be to reduce pollution as close to source as possible.

First flush

Paved areas quickly acquire a covering of silt and pollutants from atmospheric deposits, vehicles, spills, sprays and litter. When it rains heavily enough, this material starts to be washed off the paved area and into the drainage system. The polluted runoff from a small sub-catchment occurs near the beginning of the rainfall event. This is known as the first flush.

> **Treatment volume (Vt):** an estimate of the volume of runoff that contains the most polluted part of the runoff from a storm.

The insoluble pollutants will be mobilised only when the rainfall intensity reaches a threshold that both loosens the material and also exceeds the infiltration capacity of the ground, leading to surface runoff. The runoff needs to be fast enough to transport the sediments, so pollutants might not be flushed out of the system in a single event. Pollutants can therefore accumulate at one location before being washed out during a major storm.

When the flow from several sub-catchments combines, the variation in pollutant load will depend on the size of the catchment, the land use, the time of concentration, the permeability of the soil and the rainfall characteristics.

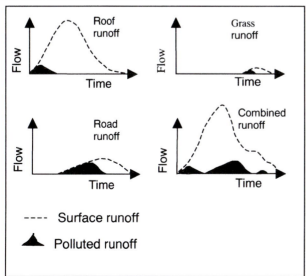

---- Surface runoff

▲ Polluted runoff

Hydrograph showing the first flush of a storm in a mixed surface catchment

When designing drainage systems for treatment, it is important to capture as much of the polluted water as possible. The volume that has to be captured is called the **treatment volume (Vt)**. This retains the most polluted water from the start of large storms or throughout the whole of smaller events. The remainder of runoff can be routed through devices to manage the flows. Some devices (infiltration trenches, filter drains) are sized on flow quantity criteria that is in excess of treatment volumes, and so these do not have to be specifically designed for quality considerations. Swales, basins and ponds that are being designed primarily for treatment will need to be sized to capture the treatment volume.

There are several methods of determining the treatment volume for basins. These include:

◆ 12-15 mm runoff distributed over each contributing sub-catchment area

◆ 12-15 mm runoff distributed over the contributing impervious catchment area

◆ the volume of runoff generated from the mean annual storm over the total catchment area or the contributing impervious catchment area

◆ a volume that would capture the runoff from 90 per cent of storms occurring in a year (this could be reduced to 75 per cent if the sub-catchment is small, uniform and has a limited pollution potential).

The methods are listed in order of increasing requirements for rainfall and catchment data. An example of the 90 per cent volume is provided in Appendix C. All the runoff being routed through the treatment facility will need to be included.

17

If a sub-catchment is a mixture of impervious and vegetated areas, the runoff from the vegetated area will still be routed through a treatment stage, even though it may not need it. To avoid oversizing the drainage device, the runoff from sub-catchments with less than 5 per cent impermeable area can be directed along a different route from potentially polluted flows. For further information see *The design of flood storage reservoirs* (CIRIA, 1993).

Treatment processes

The pollutants found in surface runoff can include:

- inorganic particles (sands, silts)

- organic particles

- heavy metals and toxic compounds

- materials in suspension

- dissolved matter

- floating solids (litter)

- oils and chemicals.

Water can be polluted from a variety of sources

Treatment can be achieved by methods such as:

- filtration through a bed of filter medium, in soils or across a vegetated area

- physical settlement in a slow-moving or still water body

- biological treatment by micro-organisms growing on filter media, soil particles, vegetation or suspended in a water body

- adsorption of particles on plants or filter media

- dilution for the control of non-persistent pollutants.

The treatment should be arranged so that coarse particles are removed before settling or filtering finer material. Once this has been achieved, biological treatment can take place without overloading the treatment facility.

The amount of treatment necessary will depend on the forecast level of pollutants. Different treatment mechanisms have different impacts on the water quality. Thus an extended detention basin should store the treatment volume for between 15 and 24 hours to remove coarse sediments; a retention pond should store the volume for two to three weeks to also remove fine sediments and organic material. Retention ponds have to have a volume of about four times the treatment volume, while wetlands, which are more efficient in removing pollutants, need up to two weeks retention time and a volume of two to three times the treatment volume.

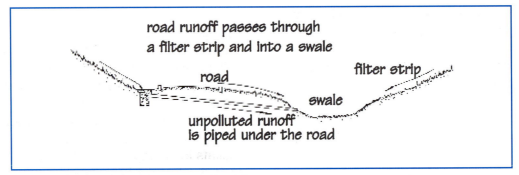

Routing unpolluted runoff separately can reduce treatment volumes, but the piped flow should be spread along the side of the swale

Amenity considerations

Amenity covers a wide range of issues that can broadly be divided into:

♦ water as a resource

♦ amenity for the local community

♦ provision of wildlife habitats.

Water as a resource
Traditionally in the UK, rainwater has been considered a waste product rather than a resource. This attitude is changing, as water is now a commodity, with an associated price. Reuse of rainwater is an aspect of SUDS that will become increasingly valuable.

Amenity for the local community
SUDS offer the opportunity to improve facilities for the local population. Amenity considerations are site-specific, but some of the issues that could be discussed with planners and landscape architects include:

♦ recreational uses of SUDS as part of open space requirements

♦ opportunities for education

♦ potential multiple uses of SUDS (eg permeable paving for car parks and infiltration basins for sports pitches)

♦ levels of landscape maintenance

♦ visual impact

♦ topography

♦ site layouts

♦ water features, including the use of ponds for amenity where they may not be required for treatment or attenuation

♦ points where roads and footpaths cross linear drains such as swales.

Drainage features can be designed to suit a variety of landscape styles

Wildlife habitats
SUDS can improve wildlife habitat. Ponds and wetlands offer the greatest opportunity, with aquatic and emergent vegetation providing a habitat for fish, amphibians, reptiles, birds and mammals. Grassed surfaces in filter strips, swales and infiltration basins can be integrated into general landscaping, and can be used to create green corridors, linking to wildlife habitats elsewhere.

Drainage facilities can provide niche habitats for flora and fauna

The design of SUDS should aim to maximise species diversity. Local grasses, flowers and wetland vegetation should be used wherever possible. When designing ponds and wetlands, use complex rather than single water bodies, and vary the depth, type of vegetation, pool size and water permanence. This will provide a variety of habitats for a range of wildlife. More details on designing for wildlife are given in the detailed design sections.

Other design considerations

Many factors (technical, environmental and management-related) determine the final choice of drainage system.

Integration of design
Drainage systems should consider issues of runoff quantity, quality and amenity, but should also be integrated with other parts of the built environment. Drainage near roads should ensure not only that the surface can shed water quickly, but also that the ground around the roads and paths should not become saturated. Lack of free draining of the ground under the road can lead to loss of ground strength and frost heave. If drainage runs alongside roads, the carriageway will need to be defined and measures taken to avoid over-running or parking on verges.

The relative position of the drainage to roads, paths, driveways, street furniture, structures and public utilities should be considered, especially where they cross drainage routes. If the catchment contains piped surface water drainage, this should be considered in detail.

This swale in Perthshire has been stepped to ensure slow flows in the individual sections of the channel

Topography
The topography of the site will determine the size and shape of sub-catchments, and might also influence the type of drainage devices selected. In natural drainage systems, for example, wetlands form on flat sites and fast-flowing streams are found in steeply sloping areas.

The versatility of SUDS allows them to be used in a variety of topographies. For example, swales can be used on steep sites by following the contours. By contrast, at Gallows Knowe in Dunning, Perthshire, a swale serves a steep site by being designed as a "waterfall", with shallow swales connected by vertical gabion walls.

Scale
By dividing the area to be drained into sub-catchments, all sites can be treated as a collection of small areas. By using source control for each sub-catchment, a large site can use the same drainage methods as an individual plot. If source control cannot be used, sub-catchments have to be grouped together and the runoff managed on a site or regional level.

Management
The future management of the site can influence the choice of drainage system. A single soakaway per household is easier to manage than a communal soakaway that needs shared ownership and maintenance.

At sites where ground staff are employed, grass mowing and maintenance of swales, filter strips and basins will take place regularly. At other sites, it may be preferable to contract out maintenance work, so annual maintenance of pavements, basins or ponds might be more appropriate.

Education
The first method of managing water quantity and quality is prevention. To promote responsible use of the drainage system, education of the occupiers of the site in good housekeeping is a key component of site management.

Institutions and single-owner sites have an advantage in being able to plan and implement education programmes more effectively than a multi-occupancy site. The impact of the change in attitude to site drainage can also be assessed more readily.

Costs and benefits

In selecting a design from a series of options, the cost will be considered and a cost-benefit analysis should be carried out.

Relevant costs include land take, the whole-life costs (construction, operation, maintenance, and possible replacement) and other costs associated with the system.

If a drainage system incorporates a significant landscape component, then this should be recognised when comparing it with systems that do not have this dual role. The whole system, rather than individual components, should be costed. A permeable pavement might be more expensive than an impermeable surface, but the picture might change when the costs of additional construction, gullies, drains, manholes and treatment facilities are included.

The issues of whole-life costing, environmental economics, cost-benefit and cost-effective analysis are explored in *Sustainable urban drainage systems – best practice*. Planners should aim to ensure that the development does not impose undue external costs on other stakeholders.

Safety

Safety reviews have to be considered site by site. All drainage techniques have advantages and risks, and a balance must be struck. For example, culverts are confined spaces, whereas swales have sloping sides. Which technique is safer depends on the site itself.

The risks associated with open water features can be minimised by community education and careful design – for example the use of shallow planted margins.

It is recommended that consultation with RoSPA is carried out if there are specific safety concerns.

18

Access to a water feature might be encouraged for education and recreation, and measures taken at particular areas to ensure this is safe. In other areas, access could be discouraged by the use of barrier planting, notices or low permanent fencing. Barrier planting has advantages over fencing as it has visual and wildlife value as well as being more of a deterrent than a challenge to unwanted visitors.

Monitoring

Checking that the more natural drainage techniques are working correctly is difficult unless monitoring facilities are incorporated at the design stage. These may be used by the body carrying out the maintenance to ensure that the level of work is correct and by the regulator to assess whether the design criteria are being achieved.

Safety is an issue not just for ponds, but also inlets and outlets

Example

This example illustrates the use of the selection tool to produce the design of a drainage system using SUDS. The level of detail is suitable for submission with a planning application. Other information that is required for such an application includes layout drawings, plans and cross-sections of the drainage design, landscape drawings and maintenance schedules.

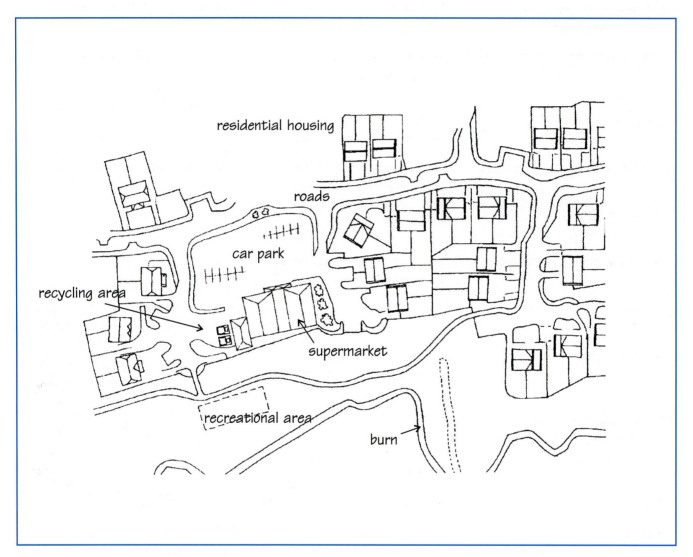

All site characteristics are fictional, and are used only to illustrate the process.

The designers initially have to assess the site and gather relevant data. This is collated in the information checklist in Appendix B.

Description	Details for the particular project	Consultees and sources of information
Existing topography	Flat area near a burn	Site inspections, local authority plans
Details of receiving sewer/ watercourse/aquifer	The burn is not to be adversely affected by flows or quality of runoff	Water authority, SEPA, local authority
Quantity/discharge design criteria	Flow into burn restricted to 20 l/s in any storm event	Water authority, SEPA, local authority
Quality design criteria, level of treatment	All roofs: one level of treatment; roads and car park: two levels; recycling area: three levels	Water authority, SEPA, local authority
Rainfall data (preferably recorded)	None available – use Wallingford Procedure Volume 3 maps	Met Office, site observations
Hydrology of catchment (including greenfield runoff)	Not available	Site observations
Soil type and infiltration potential	Soil type 4. Tests indicate negligible infiltration potential	Site tests
Environmentally sensitive areas	None	SEPA, local authority, Scottish Natural Heritage
Development type, land use	4 ha infill site. 60 houses, a supermarket, car park and recycling centre	Client, engineer, planner and regulator
Size of entire catchment, likely impermeable areas	4 ha total. House roofs 0.5 ha, gardens 1 ha, roads and car park 0.8 ha, supermarket roof 0.3 ha, recycling 0.2 ha, soft areas 1.2 ha	Client, engineer, planner and landscape architect
Availability and cost of land	Land already owned by client	Client and planner
Sub-catchment types within development	Residential (houses), commercial (roads, supermarket and car park), industrial (recycling)	Client, engineer, planner and regulator
Proposed topography	Similar to existing. Play area planned close to burn to provide flooding buffer	Client, engineer, planner, SEPA, local authority, landscape architect
Amenity provision	Playing fields/recreational area required. Gardens and landscaping in car parks	Local authority, landscape architect, local residents and pressure groups
Ecology, wildlife habitat provision	Any provision of wildlife habitat is welcomed	SEPA, wildlife protection groups, Scottish Natural Heritage
Health and safety considerations	All sightlines to be kept clear. Flotation aids and signs to be installed at burn	All affected parties

General design points

1. From the Information Checklist, the general approach will be to separate the site into three sub-catchments and consider them individually with regard to drainage.

   Having identified some possible solutions for each, review the whole system to explore the possibility of integration.

2. To protect the burn from erosion and avoid potential flooding downstream, discharge from the site is limited to 20 l/s in any storm. A critical duration of 60 minutes is considered reasonable in the absence of any site-specific flow and rainfall data.

3. Infiltration tests indicate that the soil is not suitable for disposal of water by infiltration.

4. A range of storm events should be considered to ascertain likely minimum and maximum flows. Return periods of one, five, ten and 100 years have been selected, each of 60 min duration.

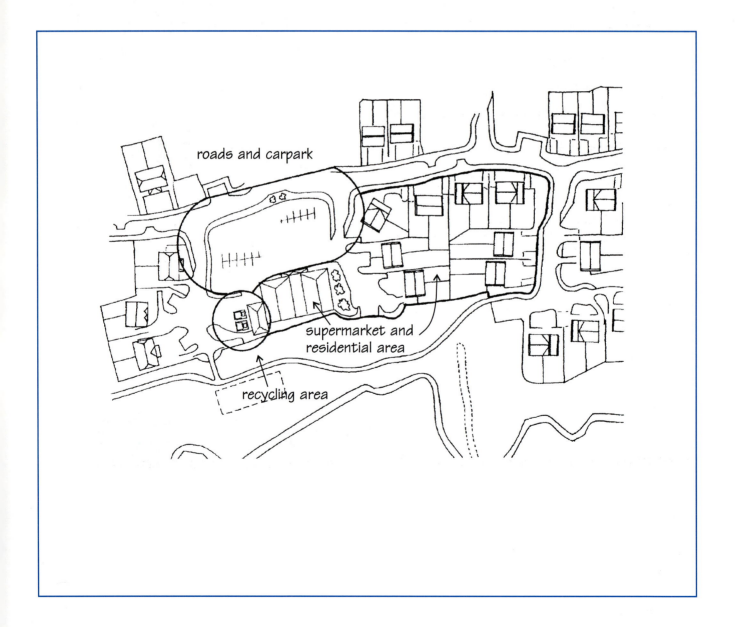

Calculation of flows from the different areas

The flow into the burn should be restricted to 20 l/s in any storm event. For sizing of drainage devices, a criterion of zero flooding in a five-year storm event has been taken as the design parameter. Checks will be made for more severe events to ensure that flooding levels remain acceptable.

Total impermeable area	=	1.8 ha
Maximum flow from site	=	20 l/s

Maximum flow apportioned to each sub-catchment:

house roofs	–	5.6 l/s
roads	–	4.4 l/s
car park	–	4.4 l/s
supermarket	–	3.3 l/s
recycling area	–	2.2 l/s

Move to the selection tool for each sub-catchment.

Houses

Quality	A residential area, so only one level of treatment is required by the regulator.
Quantity	Attenuation to reduce flow to 5.6 l/s = 65 m³

Prevention
Storage in gutters is not recommended by Building Control in Scotland, but the impact of directly drained areas could be minimised by using water-butts.

1.1 m³ of water-butt storage per house would be adequate to contain a five-year return period storm. This option would fail if the water-butts were not emptied regularly.

Source control
Infiltration is not possible; we are looking for one level of treatment as well as attenuation of 65 m³ and conveyance of the runoff for disposal.

There are many possible options for source control, including:

🔹 swales along roads collecting roof drainage and piping it to the burn

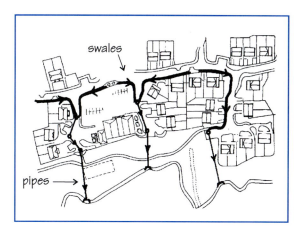

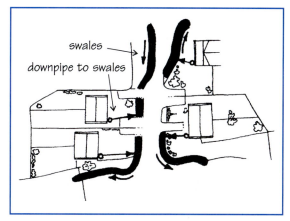

Does this satisfy the design criteria ? → **No – move to source control**

- oversized pipes discharging via a spreading device to a swale and running to the burn

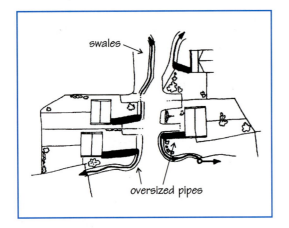

- filter drains from houses connecting to road drainage (drains should have an impermeable liner if <5 m from buildings)

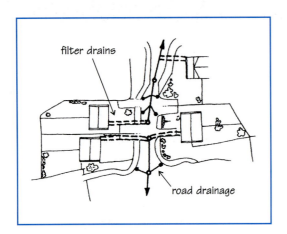
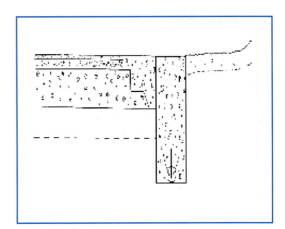

- permeable paving for driveways, conveying roof drainage to roads.

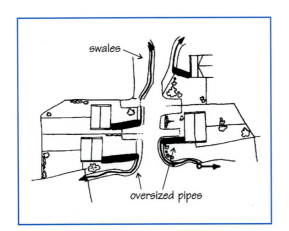
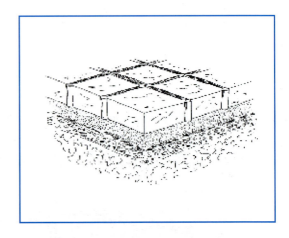

Does this satisfy the design criteria ?   Yes – investigate these options

Source control satisfies the design criteria for the house roofs, so there is no need to go further down the decision tool.

Roads and car park

Quality   Two levels of treatment are required by the regulator. Although only one level of treatment may be suitable for some of the minor roads, the proximity of the burn leads to two levels being required throughout the site.

Quantity   Attenuation to reduce flow to 4.4 l/s = 105 m³ in total.

Prevention
The roads and car park should be regularly swept and kept free of litter.

Source control
There are many possible options for source control, including:

♦ filter strips and treatment swales along roads collecting road and car park drainage and attenuating it before discharging to the burn

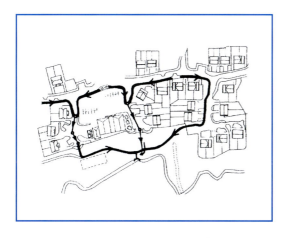

♦ permeable paving on the edge of the car park, along private roads and under the private footpaths to provide the first level of treatment. Flows pass to a basin or wetland for second level of treatment

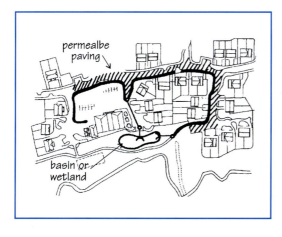
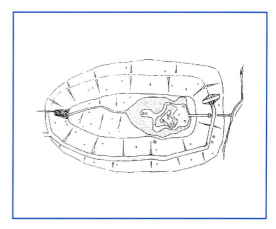

- porous paving for car park passing to a basin or wetland for the second level of treatment

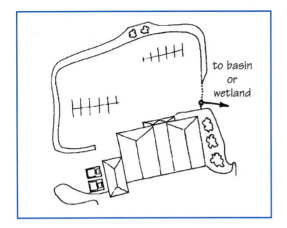

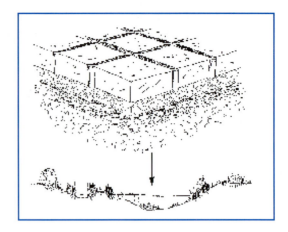

- conventional road drainage (perhaps using oversized pipes to attenuate the flow) before discharging to a filter drain or swale via a structure to spread the flow for a first level of treatment, and a basin or wetland for the second.

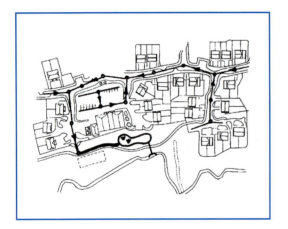

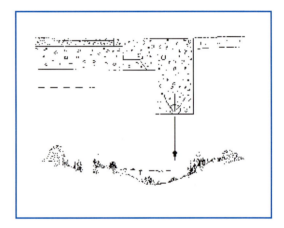

Filter strips and swales take up a lot of space, so they might not be the best solution. Permeable surfaces are currently not considered suitable for adoptable roads, so this solution is not acceptable. All the other combinations require some form of site control to provide the second level of treatment, so consider this in conjunction with site control.

| Does this satisfy the design criteria ? | No – move to site control |

Site control
The first level of treatment is provided by source control. An extended detention basin or wetland is required to provide the second level of treatment. Part of the play area could be utilised for the extended detention basin. As the basin would be wet for part of the year, a safety assessment would clearly be required.

A wetland is preferred for its landscape value and provision of wildlife habitat. This would be a permanent feature, located in the recreation area. Safety would be easier to ensure, as the area would not be put to any other use. Wetlands require a minimum flow, so check that there is sufficient connected area to maintain the wetland.

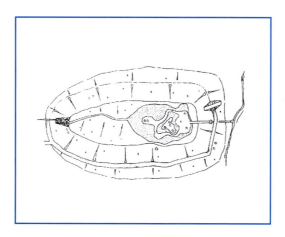

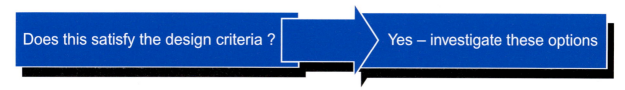

Does this satisfy the design criteria ? Yes – investigate these options

A combination of source and site control satisfies the criteria for both roads and car park. There is no need to go further down the decision tool.

Supermarket roof
Quality   One level of treatment is required by the regulator.

Quantity   Attenuation to reduce flow to 3.3 l/s = 40 m^3.

Prevention
Storage in gutters is not recommended by Building Control in Scotland, but directly drained area could be minimised by using a tank of volume 40 m^3 to contain a five-year return period storm.

This option would fail if the water was not reused.

Does this satisfy the design criteria ? No – move to source control

Selecting SUDS

Source control
Infiltration is not possible, so we are looking for one level of treatment as well as attenuation of 40 m^3 and conveyance.

There are many possible options for source control, including:

- connecting roof drainage into the car park drainage system by traditional pipes, or

- filter drains from the supermarket connecting to the car park drainage (drains should have an impermeable liner if <5 m from buildings)

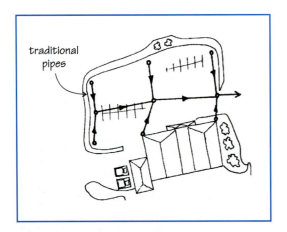 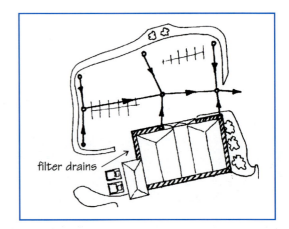

- oversized pipes discharging to a swale and running to the burn.

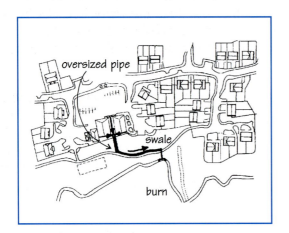 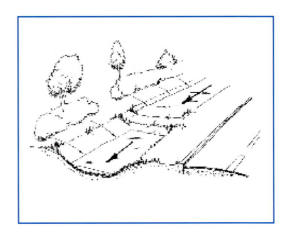

Does this satisfy the design criteria ? → Yes – investigate these options

Source control satisfies the design criteria for the supermarket roof, so there is no need to go further down the decision tool.

Recycling area

Quality   Three levels of treatment are required by the regulator.

Quantity   Attenuation to reduce flow to 2.2 l/s= 26 m^3.

Prevention

It might be possible to separate the skip area from the vehicle turning area, but the risk of pollution is too high. Treat the whole recycling area as one unit and bund it to contain any pollution. Runoff will then be passed to the foul sewer. A vortex control may be able to provide the some attenuation in order not to surcharge the foul sewer.

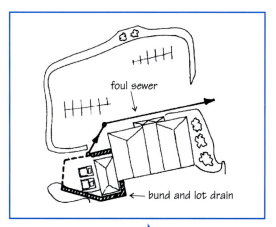

Does this satisfy the design criteria ?	Yes – negotiate a consent

This option satisfies the design criteria, so long as the water authority accepts the foul discharge. There is no need to go further down the decision tool at this stage.

Other possible solutions to the drainage of the skip area that would give the required three levels of treatment are:

- area drains to a settling basin (covered); flows are conveyed to a wetland via swales

- runoff flows to a settling basin via a gravel filter strip and then drains to a wetland.

Review entire system

The layout of the site is such that filter strips and swales would use up a lot of space, so filter drains or pipes may be preferable. A wetland is recommended for its landscape, wildlife and treatment potential. An extended detention basin offers similar benefits, but consideration must be given to the safety issues. Use of permeable pavements must be restricted to the car park, as they are not currently considered suitable for adoptable roads. Infiltration drainage is not considered suitable for this site.

There are four possible surface water drainage system for the site:

- The roof drainage from the supermarket drains to the car park, which is paved with porous blocks. This flows to filter drains, which also take the water from the house roofs and convey it to an extended detention basin. The skip area is bunded and drains to the foul sewer.

- The flows from the car park and supermarket roof enter filter drains and flow to swales along the roads. The swales also take the residential flows and road drainage and drain to a wetland. The skip area flows to a covered settling basin, then joins the swale system to be conveyed to the wetland.

- Runoff from the residential housing and supermarket roofs are taken via swales to the burn. Conventional pipes take the flows from the road and car park via a spreading device to a separate swale, which drains to an extended detention basin. The skip area drains to the foul sewer.

- The roof drainage from the supermarket and the residential area runs by filter drain into the stream. The car park is surfaced with porous paving and flows from the sub-base to join the filter drain system. The road drainage is piped to a separate filter drain, which then flows to a wetland. The skip area drains through a gravel filter strip into a covered settling basin before draining to the wetland.

Capacities and flooding check
Flooding
For each solution it is necessary to check the storage capacity to ensure it is sufficient.

Base flows to wetland
Similarly, for those solutions involving a wetland, it is necessary to ensure that the base flows will be sufficient to keep it wet throughout the year.

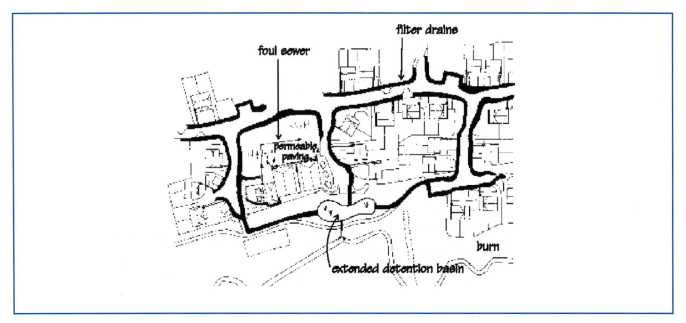

Solution 1

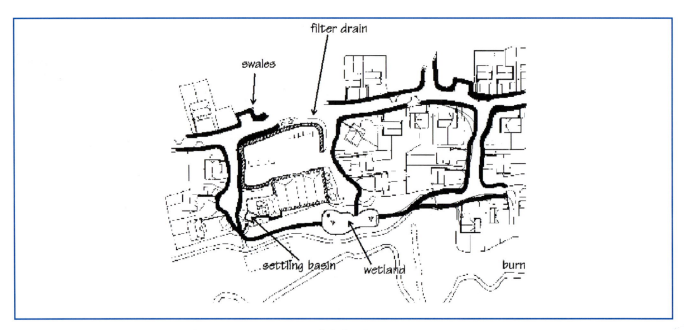

Solution 2

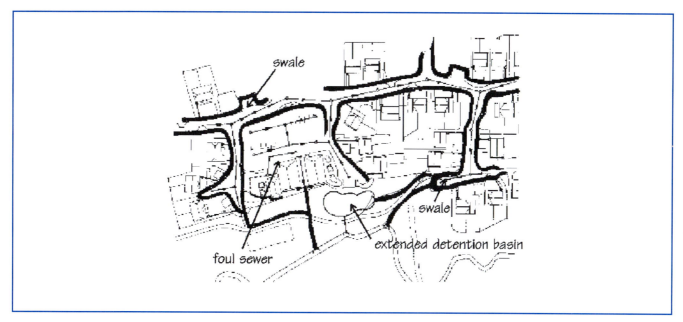

Solution 3

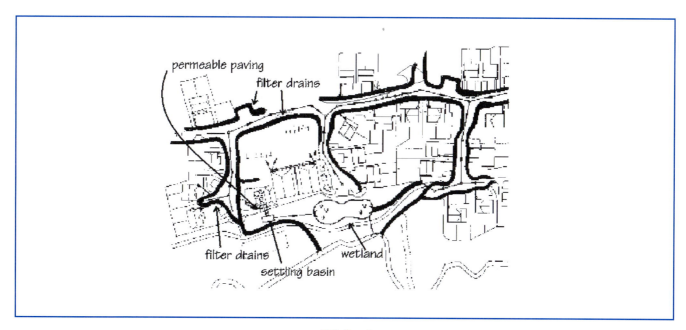

Solution 4

5 Designing SUDS

The following sections give advice on some of the current best practice in designing sustainable urban drainage systems. This is a large topic and references are given to sources of more detailed guidance where this is required. Conventional hydraulics can be used for the design of many devices, and this is adequately covered in standard textbooks.

The techniques introduced in this section cover the more natural drainage devices. Other devices that could be used as part of a drainage system include variations on traditional methods such as storage pipes and control structures, as well as proprietary products such as vortex control devices and oil separators.

Although the techniques are discussed individually it should be remembered that the drainage should operate as an integrated system, with devices working in series or parallel. For example coarse sediment should be removed by routing the runoff over a filter strip before it enters a filter drain or infiltration trench, to prevent the voids within the device being blocked. Flow can be directed through a detention pond to remove sand before entering a wetland; this will reduce the need to remove sediment from the wetland and concentrate the material in an area where it can be easily removed in dry conditions. A large swale may be needed in parallel with the wetland to route excessive runoff around the device.

The methods discussed in this section are arranged in the order they should be used in the surface water management train, rather than the four general groups discussed in Chapter 2.

Device	Filter strips and swales	Filter drains and permeable surfaces	Infiltration devices	Basins and ponds
Prevention	Used with all devices			
Permeable pavements		*	(*)	
Filter strips	*			
Swales	*		*	
Soakaways and infiltration trenches			*	
Filter drains		*		
Infiltration basins			*	
Detention basins				*
Retention ponds				*
Wetlands				*

This basin east of Dunfermline was constructed in advance of the main development so that it could become established before receiving large quantities of runoff

Preventative measures

When applying the philosophy of sustainable urban drainage, the adage "prevention is better than cure" can make practical economic sense. Managing the site can significantly reduce quality and quantity problems, and can improve amenity. Site management includes design and maintenance as well as the education of users.

Minimising runoff

Minimising paved areas
Runoff increases in proportion to the impervious area of the site. If the site is similar to its greenfield state, the runoff will also be similar. If less than 5 per cent of a site is paved or compacted, the impact on the quantity of the surface runoff will be negligible. The use of gravel limits the impervious area and gravelled surfaces can replace tarmac in parking areas on domestic driveways.

Reducing the amount of runoff also reduces the washoff of pollutants. **Rainwater recycling** can remove runoff from the drainage system altogether.

> **Rainwater recycling:** collection and reuse of rainwater runoff within a development site.

Minimising directly connected areas
Hard paving and roofed areas can be drained onto unpaved areas. Driveways and footpaths can be drained onto surrounding lawns.

The surface water management train advocates the return of runoff to the natural drainage system as soon as possible.

Good housekeeping

The amount of pollution in the first flush of a storm can be minimised by keeping paved areas clean. Maintenance measures such as sweeping hard surfaces regularly can reduce pollution. Preventing the accumulation of contaminants is even more effective. For example, placing canopies over areas of potentially high contamination removes the risk of surface water runoff becoming polluted. Good housekeeping can be made easier by using proprietary systems. Silt traps, downpipe filters and petrol separators can be used to treat runoff before it reaches the drainage system.

Education
Informing and educating users of the site about the way the site is drained can help prevent contaminants from entering the drainage system. Pollutants that need to be controlled include:

- car oil and antifreeze
- detergents (from car washing)
- household chemicals
- garden chemicals.

Water butts can provide offline attenuation for downpipes, minimising the impact of runoff from roofs

These should be used carefully and disposed of properly, not poured down surface water drains. Fertilisers, herbicides and pesticides should be used sparingly, in accordance with manufacturers' instructions, and not used where they can be washed directly into a watercourse.

Litter and animal faeces can be kept out of drainage systems by education and provision of bins.

Minimising sources of diffuse pollution

Road sweeping
Many contaminants can be removed by regular sweeping, before they are washed into the drainage system. Washing often moves the polluted material further along the drainage system where it might be more difficult to control. *Sediment management in urban drainage catchments* (CIRIA, 1995) provides further information.

Wrong connections
Connecting foul sewers to the surface water system causes pollution. The use of swales and permeable surfaces can limit these misconnections by replacing underground surface water drains because there are no surface water pipes to connect to. If a foul connection is made to a SUDS, the source of pollution soon becomes apparent.

Roads
Preventative measures include good practice during cleaning, winter maintenance and general maintenance. See *Control of pollution from highway drainage discharges* (CIRIA, 1994) for more information.

Containment
Some substances are so polluting that special measures must be taken to contain them and stop them reaching the drainage system. Risk assessments must be made and appropriate bunds and treatment facilities provided. Further details are given in the *Design of containment systems for the prevention of water pollution from industrial incidents* (CIRIA, 1997). Oil separators are discussed in the prevention guidelines PPG3 (SEPA).

Permeable surfaces

Permeable surfaces are load-bearing constructions surfaced with materials that allow surface water to enter the underlying construction. The surfacing material can itself be porous (made up of a matrix of interlinked pores that allows ingress of water), or water can enter the sub-base through joints and spaces between impermeable blocks. The important aspect of permeable surfaces is that runoff is stored and conveyed through the sub-base construction. Permeable surfaces remove the need for traditional drainage ancillaries such as gully pots and manholes and can be used as attenuation or infiltration devices. Permeable surfaces are currently not considered suitable for adoptable roads.

Design

There are three elements in the design of permeable surfaces:

- surfacing material

- underlying construction layers (eg sub-base) where the runoff is stored

- supporting soil (sub-grade).

The design of these elements is determined by the use to be made of the pavement and its expected operational life.

The types of surfacing material should be selected to suit the location and use of the area. Visual appearance may be the determining factor. An example describing the factors that might govern the choice of pavement is given in the Appendix C. Types of surfacing include:

- grass (if the area will not be trafficked)

- reinforced grass

- gravelled areas

- solid paving blocks with large vertical holes filled with soil or gravel

- solid paving blocks with gaps between the individual units

Gravel creates permeable surfaces, minimising runoff

- **porous paving** blocks with a system of voids within the unit

- continuous surfaces with an inherent system of voids

> **Porous paving:** pavement surfaces with networks of small pores (such as no-fines concrete pavers and porous asphalt) are often referred to as porous pavements.

The sub-base supporting the surface material can be constructed from materials such as:

- local subsoil (if suitable)

- sands and gravel

- layers of imported crushed stone

- suitable recycled aggregate.

The nature and depth of construction is dependent upon the design use for the pavement. More guidance can be found in the *Specification for highway works* and manufacturers' literature. There is currently no specific design guidance for the selection of high-voids sub-base material.

Correctly selected geotextiles may be used to separate construction layers, reinforce soils and maintain the natural filtration capacity of the soil, allowing infiltration in a range of soil conditions.

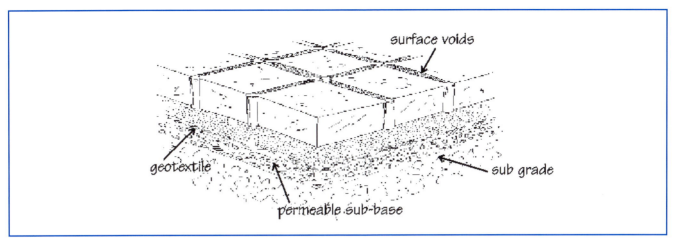

Cross-section of permeable paving

Five aspects must be considered in the design of permeable surfaces:

1. The structural strength required for the intended use (including construction loads). **Current design standards** mainly cover conventional pavement design.

2. The effective capture of surface water.

3. The discharge of the captured water through the base of the construction.

4. The internal storage volume to meet the temporary requirements for infiltration to the soil or discharge via a drain.

5. Provision of an overflow or surface storage to accommodate rainfall from storms more severe than the design event.

The relative importance of these aspects is site-specific and depends on:

◆ design uses for the pavement

◆ potential pollution problems

◆ suitability of ground conditions for infiltration

◆ the operational life expected from the pavement.

Permeable surfaces can be used to dispose of surface water runoff by infiltration into the sub-grade. This method of disposal is only suitable where the sub-grade strength will not be significantly affected by an increased moisture content. Geotextiles may be included to reinforce soils in this case.

The **current design standards** for pavements include:

Manual of contract documents for highway works Volumes 1–3, The Stationery Office:1998

Specification for paving blocks (BS6717: Part 1:1993)

Specification for pavers (BS6677: Part 1:1986)

Guide for structural design of pavements constructed with clay or concrete block pavers (BS7533: 1992)

Code of practice for laying precast concrete paving blocks and clay pavers for flexible pavements (BS7533: Part 3: 1997)

Where surfaces are designed as infiltration devices, it is important to assess the rate of soil infiltration and the minimum internal storage required. Reference to the *Groundwater protection policy for Scotland* (SEPA, 1997) should be made wherever pavements act as infiltration devices.

Permeable surface using specially shaped concrete blocks. The joints between the blocks are not filled with sand and water can percolate down to the sub-base

Designing SUDS – permeable surfaces

The soil infiltration rate should be determined at the pavement location. Refer to the section on *soakaways and infiltration trenches* for the procedure for determining the soil infiltration rate.

The sub-base of permeable surfaces can also be used to attenuate and store surface water runoff. In cases where infiltration may be undesirable (for example, where the soil is not suitable for infiltration, or the runoff is heavily polluted), the surface can be constructed with an impermeable membrane, allowing the pavement construction to act as a storage reservoir. Runoff can then be piped out for reuse or disposal by more traditional methods. Significant attenuation and improvement in quality of flows can be achieved in this manner.

Reduced outflow rates can be achieved from a permeable surface, without any expensive or complex controls. There will be no discharge if the water is to be stored within the sub-base for reuse for such purposes as landscape watering.

Silt particles are usually an indicator of frost susceptibility, so no-fines sub-base will be less prone to damage.

Evaporation from permeable surfaces can be significant. Research indicates that up to 30 per cent of the water stored below a permeable surface is lost through evaporation.

Permeable surfaces should be as flat as possible. The water is therefore spread evenly over the surface rather than concentrating it at low points. This will help prevent blockages.

If a pavement is constructed on a slope, water flows under the surface and collects at the lowest point. If the gradient of the sub-base is greater than approximately 1 in 30, a check should be made to ensure that the pavement's storage capacity is not significantly reduced and that water will not pond and appear on the surface of the pavement. If this is likely to occur, shallow ridges can be designed across the sub-grade. These intercept internal surface flows and encourage storage for infiltration or attenuation.

Where the disposal of surface water is to a drain, the pavement is usually constructed with an impermeable liner with sealed joints. If it is necessary to prevent flow downslope, as indicated above, internal walls can be installed around contours to sub-divide the internal structure into panels. The panels are linked to allow the water to move progressively downslope, but with maximum attenuation. The release of water from a pavement system should be slow, lasting several hours.

The surface of a permeable pavement can hold significant amounts of water as surface wetting. After a period of dry weather, it may even retain storms of total depth up to 5 mm with no discharge at all. The presence of water within the construction is frequently seen as a threat to the integrity of the structure during cold weather when temperatures fall to freezing. In practice, there is no history of problems caused by heave or cracking.

Research shows that the air within a permeable pavement structure retains heat for many days. Only when air temperatures at the ground remain below zero for at least two weeks will the air within the sub-base approach freezing. The absence of fine material within the construction means that there are large voids in both the surface and the sub-base. In traditional pavements with smaller voids the expansion of ice causes heave in the structure. In permeable pavements, expansion of the ice takes place into the air voids, and the structure remains intact.

Temperature variation in a permeable pavement cross-section

It is recommended that the effects of frost heave are considered on any material within 450 mm of the surface. Salt and grit for de-icing may not be needed, and this should be considered carefully in the maintenance of permeable surfaces.

Light loading permeable paving in Edinburgh

Light loading

Where permeable surfaces are subject to light loading (such as pedestrian or occasional car traffic), the pavement can be constructed on the subsoil with a thin bedding layer. Typically only 100 mm of bedding sand or gravel is required. In these circumstances, the likely effects of frost heave on the thin bedding layer and sub-grade should also be considered within 450 mm of the surface.

The use of permeable pavements designed for light loading is limited to situations where infiltration is acceptable, as there is not enough room to install a piped drainage system within the pavement structure. Consideration should be given to the economics of constructing a deeper pavement to incorporate drainage pipes.

Several commercial companies market surfacing material and systems for this style of light loading construction. Reference should be made to company literature for details of the required sub-base and construction processes.

Medium and heavy loading

Under medium and heavy traffic loading, the integrity of permeable pavement layers is important. Places where permeable pavements can be used include commercial premises and motorway service areas.

Under heavy loading, permeable paving materials require a higher quality of supporting material. The underlying construction layers should include a crushed stone sub-base. This helps to transfer traffic loading through to the sub-grade. The sub-base material should be thick enough to ensure even distribution of the construction and design loads. Again, the impact of frost heave should be considered on materials within 450 mm of the surface.

The surfacing materials used for permeable pavements subject to heavy traffic loads are:

- porous pressed concrete blocks

- solid pressed concrete blocks shaped to form voids at joints

- porous asphalt (although this is less suitable for static loads and fuel resistance).

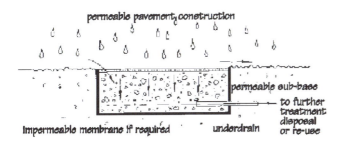

Permeable pavement used for storage

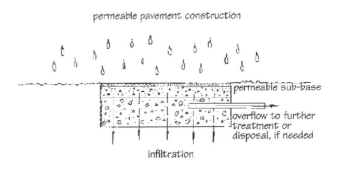

Permeable pavement used for infiltration

Certain manufacturers supply heavy-duty permeable paving systems. When designing or installing such a system, reference should be made to the manufacturers' literature for information on installation and design requirements such as:

● traffic loading limits

● maximum acceptable depth of rainfall

● construction on sloping sites

● positioning of trees and other landscape planting within a permeable pavement area.

Typical permeable pavement

Construction

The construction of permeable pavements requires the same skills as the construction of traditional pavements, but with some particular requirements:

● they can be laid without cross-falls or longitudinal gradients

● there are no ancillary drainage structures such as manholes and gully pots to work around

● they can be laid over large uniform areas, so construction plant can be used, rather than manual techniques

● the blocks are laid on materials that lie level in all weathers and moisture contents

● permeable pavements should not be used for storage of site materials, unless the surface is protected from deposition of silt and other spillages.

In general, the pavements should be constructed in a single operation, as one of the last items to be built. Landscape development should be completed before pavement construction, to avoid contamination by silt or soil from this source.

If the surface of a permeable pavement is damaged or becomes covered by silt, mud or sand, the free-draining nature of the surface is compromised or even destroyed. Surfaces draining to the pavement should be stabilised before construction of the pavement. Inappropriate construction equipment should be kept away from the pavement to prevent damage to the surface, sub-base or sub-grade.

If it is necessary to use permeable pavements as temporary storage areas, care should be taken to protect the surface, or reinstate the free-draining characteristics of the pavement before the construction is completed.

Safety

The safety considerations for permeable pavements are similar to those for traditional pavements. The general operation of pavements presents few safety hazards. In fact, the reduced likelihood of frost or ice on the surface and the absence of manholes and gully pots reduce potential trip and slip hazards.

Surfacing materials for permeable pavements vary from rough to smooth. Where the use of pushchairs or trolleys is anticipated, a smooth surface finish should be chosen.

Care should be taken in the location of surface inlets to minimise the trip hazard for pedestrians.

Hazards associated with maintenance should be assessed site by site.

During construction, any cables, pipelines or other services located below the surface should be identified. The potential safety hazards inherent in locating services in an area used for infiltration should be considered. If a potential hazard exists, services should be protected or moved.

Operation and maintenance

If permeable pavements are used to drain adjacent roofs or impermeable areas, sediment should not be allowed to enter the pavement and block the pores. This can be prevented by passing runoff from adjacent areas through screens (on roof downpipes) or through vortex filters or gully silt traps (on paved surfaces). Water from these sources can be piped into the sub-base of the pavement, avoiding any risk of ponding on the surface.

Maintenance of permeable pavements falls into two categories:

- regular maintenance

- remedial maintenance.

Regular maintenance
Regular maintenance of the pavements is limited to surface treatment. Vacuum sweeping should be carried out twice a year:

- at the beginning of spring, when general landscape tidying of winter damage is undertaken

- in the autumn, after leaf fall.

Between sweeping cycles, general good housekeeping should minimise the impact of nearby activities. If weed control is necessary, manual control or non-toxic and biodegradable weedkillers should be used.

People working on or using permeable pavements should be made aware of their general environmental responsibility. Displaying a clear public notice to this effect will encourage responsible behaviour, and increase the awareness of SUDS.

If the surface is chosen correctly, its free-draining characteristics coupled with the lag in temperature change within the pavement should reduce the need for de-icing salts or gritting. Use of salt or grit should be avoided because these impair the flow of water through the surface and unnecessarily contribute to pollution. A risk assessment should be undertaken before considering a policy of no salting or gritting.

Remedial maintenance
Where areas of the pavement show decreased infiltration, they might require remedial maintenance. Initially the porous surface or the inlets to the permeable pavement sub-base should be cleaned or individual areas treated.

If this process fails to produce satisfactory results it will be necessary to lift the surfacing materials, possibly remove and replace the bedding gravel and reinstate the surface.

For permeable pavements with large voids (such as gravel surfaces or open-cell concrete), this process is not particularly time-consuming, onerous or expensive, and surface materials may be reused several times. However, when porous concrete or porous asphalt becomes blocked, the surface will normally need to be replaced with new porous blocks or porous asphalt.

Permeable paving is ideal for car parks

Data on the operating life of permeable pavements is limited. Current experience suggests that they might operate with limited maintenance for 15-20 years. Life expectancy will increase in situations where the site environment is maintained to a high standard.

Amenity

Permeable pavements provide amenity by combining drainage with a surface that can be used as a road, car park or storage area. There is a wide choice of surfacing materials, so colours and textures can be chosen to suit the visual environment.

The water that can be stored in the sub-base of a permeable pavement can also be used as a resource.

Trees and shrubs can be incorporated into permeable paved areas. Trees can reduce the intensity of rainfall, provide shade for parking areas and enhance the disposal of water by evapotranspiration. Tree roots can be watered by runoff stored in the sub-base, but should be carefully contained.

Filter strips

A filter strip is an area of vegetated land through which runoff is directed. It usually lies between a hard-surfaced area and a receiving stream, surface water collector or disposal system. Filter strips can be in any natural vegetated form, from grass verge to shrub areas.

To be effective, filter strips should be between 6 m and 15 m wide. The wider the strip and the more dense the vegetative cover, the better the pollutant removal, the more impact on flows and the higher the potential for amenity enhancement.

Design

Filter strips can be designed using simple hydraulic equations such as Manning's formula. The effectiveness of a filter strip as a pollutant-removal device depends on its longitudinal and cross slopes. The gentler the slope, the greater its effectiveness. Excessive slopes increase flow velocities and reduce the ability of the filter strip to trap and remove pollutants.

Pollutant-trapping efficiency is also affected by the characteristics of the vegetation – including its height, stiffness and density of planting. This determines its interaction with the flow. The diagram and chart below show the behaviour of vegetation under various hydraulic loadings and the roughness coefficients that should be used for different lengths of grass.

Typically, short-stemmed grasses on a cross-slope of 1 in 20 would result in runoff velocities of the order of 0.2 m/s. On a 6 m-wide strip, this would trap all sand particles, but less than 50 per cent of coarse silt sediments. To trap all the coarse silt sediments the filter strip should be several tens of metres wide, or the flow velocity should be reduced by flattening the gradient or increasing the roughness.

Generally the strip should be designed so regular flowrates are below 0.3 m/s to encourage settlement, while larger storms should be below 1.5 m/s to prevent erosion.

For best performance, cross-slopes should not exceed 1 in 20. In the USA, the effectiveness of filter strips has not been established on slopes greater than 1 in 14.

The minimum flow distance across a filter strip should be 6-7 m. This is considered to be a reasonable compromise between land take and pollutant-removal efficiency. If the flow travels to an infiltration trench, this distance can be reduced to 3 m.

The use of larger plants such as shrubs and trees is possible, but the gradients have to be shallow to ensure that high flow velocities are not generated around the uneven vegetation. Because the vegetation is also less dense than a uniform grass sward, treatment efficiencies are lower, so a longer flow path is required to achieve the same reduction in silt levels. Evapotranspiration and wildlife value might be increased, however.

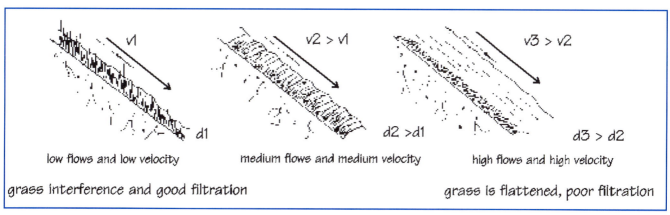

low flows and low velocity   medium flows and medium velocity   high flows and high velocity

grass interference and good filtration   grass is flattened, poor filtration

Effect of hydraulic loading on grassed surfaces

Filter strips work best under sheet flow of runoff. Details of how this can be achieved are given in the section on swale design.

An example showing the design of a filter strip and swale is given in the Appendix C.

Construction

Construction and seeding of the filter strip should be carried out early in the construction process. This allows the vegetation to become established before the filter strip comes into use.

> **Formation:** ground surface prepared to support the final surface (in this case, topsoil) to be laid.

The topsoil should be uniformly distributed and lightly compacted to a depth of 100 mm. Topsoil should not be placed while frozen or waterlogged, or when the **formation** is excessively wet. The application of seed and fertiliser should be as uniform as possible.

If the topsoil becomes dry during establishment of the vegetation, it may be necessary to irrigate the filter strip.

The permanent filter strip should be protected from traffic loading and surface water flows from the construction. It is recommended that temporary drainage systems are considered during the construction period, as the silt loadmay impair the long-term performance of the filter strip.

Safety

Although filter strips are inherently safe drainage devices, the site conditions at a particular location may require a safety review.

Amenity
Filter strips can provide green links between developments and the surrounding landscape. They are particularly applicable around the edges of car parks. In such a location, consideration should be given to installing a low-level, inconspicuous barrier to prevent unauthorised vehicular access to the filter strip. This should not, however, impede sheet flow over the strip. Trees, bollards, crash barriers or intermittently spaced boulders may be considered.

Vegetation should be selected to ensure a dense, year-round sward. Local flora should be used. Wildflower seeds may be added to the grass mixtures to increase amenity value.

Operation and maintenance

To operate effectively, filter strips rely on the following conditions:

- well-maintained grass or other vegetation able to trap pollutants

- a gently sloping site to ensure an even distribution of overland flow.

Operation of the filter strip should be checked periodically to ensure that there are:

- no rills or gullies forming across its surface

- no areas of waterlogging.

Both these conditions adversely affect a filter strip's pollutant-retaining efficiency and make access across the surface more difficult.

Maintenance of filter strips is broadly similar to general landscape maintenance. The strip should be covered uniformly with dense vegetation that develops throughout the growing season.

Grass cutting is needed to maintain a dense sward – as appropriate to the species and environmental conditions. The plant species will determine the maximum height of the sward before cutting is required. Because overland flow is shallow, increased vegetation height does not increase effectiveness. In general, the vegetation on a filter strip should be maintained at a height between 50 mm and 150 mm. Grass cuttings and leaf litter should be removed from the surface of the filter strip. Oil spills should be prevented, but they can be removed by being soaked up with absorbent materials, or can be allowed to break down in the soil.

Areas with erosion or channelisation of flows should be repaired to maintain sheet flow over the filter strip.

The treatment potential of swales and filter strips depends greatly on the type of vegetation, and this should be carefully considered. Generally, plants with flexible stems are more efficient at trapping pollutants than those with woody stems, although the density of the vegetation will have a greater effect than the type.

Salt-resistant plants might be needed in some locations. If plants cannot thrive, gravel may be used to filter the runoff and to prevent erosion.

Barriers protecting a filter drain can become part of the hard landscape

Monitoring

Regular inspections of the filter strip should be undertaken, particularly during the establishment period and after significant storm events. These inspections should:

- identify areas of erosion, scour or gullies

- determine the health of the vegetation and the soil (perhaps including a check on the level of contaminants)

- identify areas of waterlogging or other damage.

Swales

Swales are linear grassed drainage features in which surface water can be stored or conveyed. They have a significant pollutant-removal potential and can be designed to allow infiltration under appropriate conditions. They are particularly suitable for diffuse collection of surface water runoff from small residential or commercial developments, paved areas and roads.

Design

Swales can be used purely as a conveyance system. Shallow swales with relatively small longitudinal gradients are a particularly effective way of directing and conveying runoff from the drained area to another stage of the surface water management train. Deeper swales can be used for increased conveyance and storage if larger storms have to be catered for.

Swales can also be used for runoff attenuation, treatment (by settlement or filtration through the vegetation) and disposal (by allowing infiltration through the base of the swale).

A swale

A swale is a good example of the management train concept, with different functions controlling the runoff as it moves downstream. The design approach for a swale system depends upon the primary function of the swale, such as:

- conveyance
- infiltration
- treatment by detention
- treatment by filtration.

Swales to be used for conveyance should be designed in accordance with standard hydraulic principles, such as the Manning's equation discussed in the *Filter strips* section. Further information can be found in *Use of vegetation in civil engineering* (CIRIA, 1990) and the *Design of reinforced grass waterways* (CIRIA, 1987).

Ideally swales should be located alongside the impervious areas they drain so they receive sheet flow from the adjoining surface. These flows should be less than 0.3 m/s to promote filtration and settlement. Inflow to the swale should always be in sheet flow down the sides of the channel, but can be:

- through kerb cuts or a low earth weir at the edge of the swale
- via a suitable chute for surface flows from paved areas.

In these cases, the designer must take precautions to ensure that concentrated flows do not cause erosion of the swale surface.

Locating swales at the end of piped systems is not recommended, due to the high local flowrates and risk of erosion. If an underground drain does discharge into a swale, suitable scour protection and headworks will be needed to spread the flow and to trap sediment. However, directing the flow to the base of the swale bypasses the filtering effect of the side slopes.

To avoid channel erosion when the swale is at full conveyance depth, the velocity should not exceed 1.5 m/s. The longitudinal bottom slope of all types of swale should be kept as level as possible, and ideally no greater than 1 in 50.

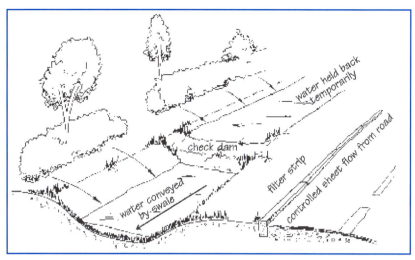

The design should promote sheet flow across a filter strip and into a swale. Check dams control the flow in the swale

Steeper overall longitudinal slopes can be accommodated by the introduction of check dam structures spaced at intervals along the length of the swale to maintain the hydraulic gradient below 1 in 50. The check dams slow down the flow, reducing erosion, and impound part of the inflow for subsequent treatment or infiltration.

Criteria for designing the check dams are as follows:

◆ they should be designed to detain the runoff upstream

◆ interconnections between adjacent **pounds** should be designed so that the flow between them does not resuspend settled material or cause local erosion

◆ interconnections between adjacent sections should be designed to retain floating solids or surface films.

> **Pound:** runoff can be temporarily impounded in swales to attenuate flows and promote settlement of solids.

If the swale is being used primarily for extended detention or infiltration it should drain the relevant design volume completely within two days. This prevents waterlogging and keeps the grass cover in good condition. After extreme storms it will obviously take longer to empty a swale, though minor events will drain quickly.

Swales need sheet flow down the sides of the device to work effectively

Swales for infiltration

The design of swales for infiltration combines the factors considered for infiltration basins and for swales used as conveyance structures. The longitudinal slope of the swale should be very gentle. Swales with a longitudinal slope in excess of 1 in 17 will not be effective for infiltration and should be treated as conveyance devices.

Because of their linear nature, swales can cover a variety of soil types across a site. It is necessary to ensure that the design soil characteristics adequately represent conditions across the site. Where there is limited ground investigation information across a site, it is advisable to dig trial pits at intervals along the length of the proposed swale. BRE Digest 365 recommends trial pits at 25 m intervals in such cases.

Swales for extended detention

Swales designed for use as water quality treatment should be capable of containing the design treatment volume (V_t) within the swale.

The swale outlet should be sized to limit the discharge of this treatment volume up to 24 hours. It can be relatively simple in hydraulic design terms – for example, a multiple small-bore-orifice outlet.

Swales for filtration

Swales can also be considered as linear filter strips, subject to the following constraints:

- the depth of flow should not exceed 0.1 m and the vegetation in the base of the swale should be maintained at or just above this notional maximum water level

- the runoff velocity in the swale should not exceed 0.3 m/s at the design treatment volume

- the base of the swale should be flat, with a smooth transition between the base and sides

- the width of the base should generally not exceed 3.0 m (this will discourage formation of gullies and ensure there is a consistent spread of flow across the swale).

When designing roadside swales in residential areas, check dam structures can conveniently be incorporated into driveway crossings or as grassed features within the swale.

The vegetation in the swale is important in preventing erosion, filtering the runoff, aiding infiltration and providing aesthetic and environmental benefits. This is an integral part of the design and measures should be taken to encourage the vegetation. Suitable grass species should be selected, taking into account the expected wear, frequency of mowing, soil type, wildlife potential and available light. Shade from trees or buildings may reduce the vigour of some species.

The landscape design should specify appropriate grass species – dense turf grass, and plants that will grow well despite periodic inundation and exposure to water flow velocities.

The sides of the swale should not be steeper than 1 in 4 to allow for mowing and access for maintenance personnel.

Construction

The bottom and side slopes of the swale should be carefully prepared to ensure that they are structurally sound, level and true and will perform their required hydraulic function. They should not be compacted during construction.

The soils used to finish the swale slopes should be suitably fertile, porous and of sufficient depth to ensure healthy vegetation growth. The use of swales in areas subject to frequent roadside parking should be avoided, as this can cause over-compaction of the soil and deterioration of the surface. Alternatively, parking can be discouraged by the use of bollards.

Swales should be integrated into the general landscaping of the site or roadside verges and protected during their construction to allow grass and plant cover to establish.

This swale is grazed by sheep to control woody plants

Operation and maintenance

Unlike infiltration devices, it is easy to see how swales are performing, which makes it simple to trace and contain pollution incidents. Swales are readily accessible for surface maintenance.

Swale systems should be inspected twice a year for signs of erosion damage, silt deposits, excessive waterlogging and poor vegetation growth. General operation and maintenance considerations are discussed under *Filter strips*.

Grass cutting should be undertaken in line with local landscape standards. Ideally, a grass height of 100 mm should be maintained. The frequency of mowing is largely dependent on the species of grass planted but is likely to be at least twice a year. More frequent mowing could be carried out for aesthetic reasons if required, but this might reduce the ability to trap silt.

Mowing and other maintenance equipment should not damage or excessively consolidate the surface. For the same reason, machines should not be used in swales when they are wet.

To maintain the grass cover on the base of the swale and to maintain good infiltration, excessive silt deposits should be removed from the surface of the swale. When this is done, the swale base should be scarified to encourage grass development.

Safety

Swales are shallow surface features that do not present significant risk or danger to the health and safety of the general public. Risks are reduced by inherent design considerations including:

◆ the shallow swale side slopes

◆ the infrequency of inundation

◆ the shallow depths of flow.

Monitoring

As for *filter strips*, regular inspections of the swale should be undertaken, particularly during the vegetation establishment period and after significant storm events.

Amenity
Swales run parallel to the areas they serve, and can form a network of green corridors, linking different areas. Such corridors are important for wildlife, act as a visual amenity and have a landscaping function.

The use of swales can improve sightlines and visibility at road junctions.

Swales are easy to integrate into general landscaping, and can be planted with trees, shrubs and local plant species.

Soakaways and infiltration trenches

Soakaways are drainage structures with a high amount of available storage. Surface water runoff can be directed to the soakaway, where the storage volume provides attenuation of the flows to allow gradual infiltration into the surrounding soil. Soakaways can be of various shapes and sizes. Long, thin soakaways are called infiltration trenches. An overflow can be provided for extreme rainfall events that exceed the storage capacity.

Design

Soakaways are a traditional form of surface water disposal for buildings and paved surfaces in free-draining ground conditions. The poor design and construction of some soakaways causes them to fail, giving soakaways a bad reputation for reliability. Properly designed and constructed soakaways work for many years.

Infiltration trenches are essentially linear soakaways. They are far less common in the UK than soakaways, mainly because of the perceived difficulties of incorporating trench systems within a site layout.

Infiltration trenches tend to require lower volumes of excavation and stone-fill material for a given surface water inflow than soakaways of a square

shape. Trench systems also provide an opportunity to redirect water to balance spare capacity in other parts of the system.

Surface water drainage into the soakaway or infiltration trench can be by surface flow through a pervious layer, or by underground drain discharge. Two forms of soakaway are common:

- a rubble- or stone-filled pit

- a precast concrete ring unit or brick chamber.

Both types provide some storage volume within the ground.

Infiltration trenches are filled with rubble or stone. The narrower they are, the more efficient they are in terms of construction cost. The width and length chosen will depend on the construction method and site layout.

There are some restrictions on the design of soakaways and infiltration trenches:

- they should not adversely affect groundwater resources

- they should not be constructed in ground where the water table reaches the bottom of the device at any time of the year

- they should not be constructed within 5 m of the foundations of buildings or under a road.

Soakaways can serve residential developments

Soakaways and infiltration trenches are generally located close to the building or paved surface being drained.

A site investigation should be carried out before starting the design of a soakaway or infiltration trench. This investigation should include:

◊ a geotechnical evaluation to determine the suitability of the soil for infiltration drainage. This is particularly important on sites where there is filled ground, as the frequent discharge of additional waters might change the soil characteristics, either chemically or structurally

◊ determination of the soil infiltration rate at the location and depth of the proposed device.

Two design parameters must be specified in order to proceed with the calculation of the required internal storage volume of the device:

◊ the rate of infiltration of water into the soil in the location and depth of the device

◊ the design storm or storms for which the device is to be sized.

Design of soakaways and infiltration trenches should be carried out in accordance with:

◊ BRE Digest 365, *Soakaway design* (BRE, 1991) or

◊ *Infiltration drainage – manual of good practice* (CIRIA, 1996).

The methods detailed in either of these two documents seek to find appropriate dimensions required for a range of ten-year return period storms. The design can be directed to determine the maximum depth, width or length of the required excavation.

The long-term performance of soakaways and infiltration trenches depends on maintaining the storage volume and keeping the voids clear. Any materials that are likely to fill the storage volume or seal the interface between the storage and the adjacent soil must be intercepted before discharge to the soakaway or trench.

The procedure for the determination of soil infiltration rate is described in BRE Digest 365, *Soakaway design* (BRE, 1991), and in *Infiltration drainage – manual of good practice* (CIRIA, 1996). The test procedures recommend that the test pit should be excavated to the same depth as the proposed soakaway and the fall in water level during tests should be observed over the full depth of expected operation of the soakaway.

The calculated value of the soil infiltration rate from such a test is considered to reflect any change in the nature of the soil with depth.

Suitable geotextiles can enhance the performance of infiltration devices. They should be selected to suit the surrounding soil particle size and permeability. Geotextiles include woven fabrics, needle-punched or chemical bonded materials, grids, or any combination of these.

The design storm rainfall at the location is determined by the methods detailed in the *Design and analysis of urban storm drainage, Volume 4: The Modified Rational Method* (Department of the Environment, 1981), adopting a return period of ten years.

Infiltration devices should be kept as shallow as possible to maximise the length of the flowpath to the water table. Surface water runoff receives more treatment the longer it spends percolating through the soil to the water table.

Construction

Soakaways and infiltration trenches should not be used for untreated drainage of construction sites, where runoff is likely to contain large amounts of silt, debris and other pollutants.

Stone-filled soakaway

An inspection tube (eg a 225 mm perforated pipe) should be directly connected to any incoming drains to allow the free overflow of water and prevent any build-up of debris at the end of the pipe. Debris may be removed periodically from the base of the inspection tube.

The cover should be convenient for access, and the provision of a **wayleave** should be considered where multiple properties discharge to a single soakaway.

> **Wayleave:** a right of access to the route of a pipeline crossing privately owned land. If the runoff is managed at source, wayleaves are not required.

Chamber soakaway

The design procedure assumes that the chamber will be positioned centrally in a square pit for ease of construction.

Infiltration trenches

The stone fill that provides the storage volume should be wrapped in a geotextile. A perforated or porous distributor pipe should be installed within the geotextile.

With long infiltration trenches it is advisable to provide inspection tubes at regular intervals along the trench. The extreme ends of the trench should be identified by inspection tube covers or other access covers. These provide confirmation of the line and may be convenient as points of inflow for intermediate connections.

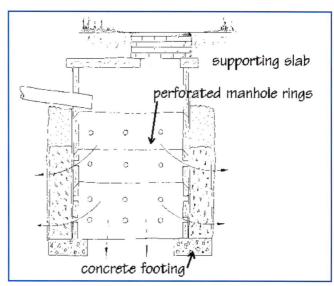

Chamber soakaway

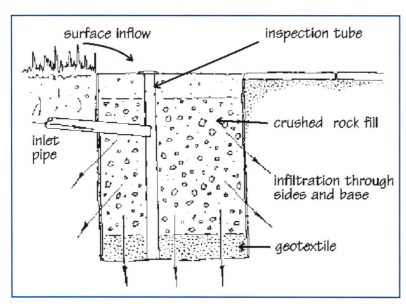

Stone-filled soakaway

Safety

Soakaways are a safe method of surface water disposal. The same applies to infiltration trenches, with the exception of possible access to a wet well, if installed. There are no surface features to attract attention, they are essentially tamper-proof and the void can be filled with stone, eliminating any danger of accidental entry. The only point of access is a small inspection cover, typically 225 mm diameter, or a cast manhole cover that requires heavy lifting gear to remove.

Properly designed soakaways and infiltration trenches are load-bearing, and can support traffic loads safely.

Collapse of soakaway and infiltration trench structures has occurred in the past, most frequently due to the surrounding soil washing into the soakaway. This can be avoided if due care is taken in the design, construction and location of soakaways.

Operation and maintenance

A problem frequently encountered with drains and sewers is the ingress of tree roots through poor joints or cracks in the pipework. Roots will be drawn to the location of a soakaway. It is unclear whether this is a benefit or problem, as the roots may provide additional pathways for water to enter the soil, and the tree will take up water itself.

> **Amenity**
> Infiltration devices, being largely underground, have a minimal visual impact on the landscape. For this reason, they can be integrated into any style of development.
>
> Infiltration assists in groundwater recharge. This can provide a benefit in watercourses suffering low flows, or can be used to help clean up already polluted groundwater.

Soakaways and infiltration trenches should be inspected annually, and maintenance undertaken as follows:

- removal of debris from the floor of inspection tube or chamber

- cleaning of filters on downpipes

- emptying of debris from any vortex filter trap or **catchpit**

- removal and washing of exposed stones on the trench surface.

> **Catchpit:** a small chamber incorporating a sediment collection sump which the runoff flows through.

Maintenance will usually be carried out by hand, although a suction tanker can be used for debris removal. A suction tanker will be required for a catch-pit. If maintenance is not undertaken for very long periods deposits might become hard-packed and require considerable effort to remove.

Replacement of the rock fill will be necessary if the device becomes blocked with silt.

An infiltration trench under construction

The area draining to an infiltration device should be swept regularly to prevent silt being washed off the surface. An alternative might be to direct the runoff across a filter strip or through an extended detention basin before it enters the infiltration device. This would remove a large proportion of the solids and minimise the risk of blockage of the infiltration device.

Filter drains

A filter drain comprises a perforated or porous pipe in a trench surrounded with a suitable filter material, granular material or lightweight aggregate fill. The fill may be exposed at the ground surface or covered with turf, topsoil or other suitable capping. Filter drains are similar to french drains.

Filter drains have been used extensively for road and car park developments, where they have been constructed in the verge and median strip. To date, they have been little used in more general conditions or within urban development.

Design

The traditional purpose of the filter drain is to intercept surface water on the verge or median strip, preventing water from entering the pavement construction formation by conveying it to a suitable discharge outlet. Some designs are provided in *Highway construction details – manual of contract documents for highway works Vol 3* (The Stationery Office).

To maximise the treatment and attenuation benefits, the perforated or porous pipe in the base should only be provided over the last few metres before the outlet, or adjacent to a manhole. The absence of a continuous drain for flows up to the design volume increases the attenuation and the potential biological treatment.

A high-level perforated pipe should be installed to provide an overflow for flows in excess of the design volume. An alternative method might be to allow the drain to back up and overflow, but the route of the floodwater should be carefully designed to avoid adverse impacts, especially frequent waterlogging of the road sub-grade.

There are advantages in establishing a network of filter drains. The high-level pipes can then be used to transfer excess waters around the system in the event of local overloading.

Typically filter drains are designed to store 10 mm of rainfall from the contributing area. Storage is provided below the high-level outlet pipe. This treatment volume is considered adequate for the compact and uniform catchments typically served by filter drains.

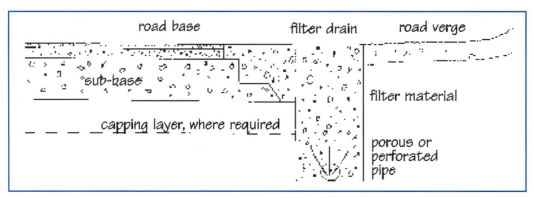

Cross-section through a filter drain

For basic design guidance, and particularly in the context of road works, reference should be made to *Highway construction details.* The drain must be designed to remove water rapidly from the sub-grade so as to protect the integrity of the pavement construction.

When considering the use of filter drains in other situations, the basic designs provided in *Highway construction details* should be adjusted to suit particular site characteristics.

Filter drains have been reported to be effective in the removal of total suspended solids (85 per cent), total lead (83 per cent), total zinc (81 per cent) and oil (estimated at around 70 per cent), annually (Perry and McIntyre, 1986).

In Sweden, filter drains are used as attenuation and treatment systems in clay soils, with the objective of maintaining soil moisture and so minimise consolidation within a newly constructed residential area.

Monitoring of discharges from a development in Göteborg, Sweden, showed that some 60 per cent of the water entering the system annually was used by plants and transpired. It thus significantly reduced the outflow to an adjacent watercourse. The filter drains were constructed under footways and car parks, and were interconnected to provide a network across the whole site.

Wider use could be made of filter drains as attenuation, treatment and conveyance systems in situations where ground conditions do not facilitate infiltration.

Filter drains can be used in the base of swales, providing extra storage and attenuation. This arrangement enhances the water quality through sedimentation in the swale and the biological treatment provided by the soil. The swale may be constructed with a flat base so that waters are stored rather than conveyed; the filter drain provides the conveyance system.

To prevent the grasses in the swale from being damaged by extended periods of immersion, stored water in the swale should discharge to the filter drain within two days. Emptying times with a combined swale/filter drain system will often be half of this discharge period.

The low-level drain is sized on the basis that it will discharge the treatment volume in 24 hours. If the drain is near a road and the sub-grade is susceptible to waterlogging, the drainage time should be reduced.

If the contributing catchment is not a uniform car park or section of road, the return period of the design storm will depend on the adjacent land use and the risks arising from failure of the system to discharge excess flows adequately.

Long-term performance of filter drains will be affected by the selection of filter material, and how effectively materials likely to fill the void space are intercepted before discharge into the drain. Where the surface water discharges to the filter drain via pipes from highway gullies or roof downpipes, silt traps or vortex-style filters should be included upstream of the filter drain.

It can be advantageous to provide a filter strip between the road pavement and the filter drain. This will aid sediment removal, and help to prevent vehicles from reaching the exposed surface of the drain when leaving the carriageway. If this is not feasible it may be necessary to build catchpits along the drain to aid maintenance.

An inspection tube, with a sealed cover allowing access for maintenance, should be provided where gullies or roof downpipes discharge to a filter drain. Typically, 225 mm perforated pipes are suitable for use as inspection tubes.

Covers should be the fire-hydrant type, if access is not required, or traditional manhole covers. The choice of cover should take into account whether it is likely to be subject to vehicle loading. Access might also be required for long-term major maintenance, so the whole length of the drain might need to be accessible.

Manholes should be installed at the junction of two filter drains, where a drain changes direction, or at maximum specified distances.

Filter drain draining a road

Construction

The Stationery Office publications *Specification for highway works and the associated Notes for Guidance (Manual of contract documents for highway works Vols 1 and 2)* should be referred to regarding details and materials.

Depending on soil type and site location, the trench may be lined with a geotextile. This should wrap over the top of the infill material to prevent ingress of soil or other surfacing material. Wherever the trench extends to the ground surface, the geotextile should be protected by 150 mm of granular or filter material.

Filter drains should not be used to drain construction sites without the runoff being pre-treated, otherwise silt will block the voids.

A filter drain using crushed rock as the filter medium

Safety

Filter drains provide an inherently safe method of surface water disposal and treatment since there is little opportunity for them to be tampered with or to attract attention.

When filter drains have filter or granular material that extends to the ground surface, there is the possibility of material being scattered when vehicles leave the carriageway. This can be minimised by the use of crushed rock for the top layer of fill material. Alternatively, porous asphalt or a layer of vegetated topsoil can be used to cover the fill material.

Operation and maintenance

Filter drains should have formal maintenance regimes in place. Maintenance requirements will be similar to those described under Soakaways. Silt traps, catchpits and other screening systems for inflows to the drain should be inspected annually and cleaned as necessary.

Where filter drains are constructed below swales, the base of the swale might require maintenance to ensure adequate infiltration into the base of the swale and hence to the filter drain.

Amenity
Filter drains remove the need for gully pots, which can become a trap for amphibians and small animals.

They can be integrated easily into the verge or median strip, and can be surfaced with materials such as asphalt, grass or gravel, thus blending into the surrounding landscape.

Infiltration basins

Infiltration basins store surface water runoff and allow it to infiltrate gradually through the soil of the basin floor. An emergency overflow can be provided for when the storage capacity of the basin is exceeded during extreme rainfall events.

Design

Infiltration basins are generally similar in cross-section to swales, with gently sloping sides and a flat base area. Whereas swales are linear features, infiltration basins may take any shape. Curving, irregular planforms are preferred from an amenity and visual standpoint.

The two main identifiable characteristics of infiltration basins are:

♦ grass cover throughout, usually maintained to the standard of the surrounding landscaping

♦ overall depths of construction ranging from 0.5 m to 3 m. A freeboard is generally retained above the maximum water level, for example 200 mm, but this should be based on an assessment of the risk of overtopping.

Inflow to the basin may be by:

♦ sheet flow down the sides

♦ a riprap or concrete chute for concentrated surface flows from paved areas

♦ a drain discharging from the side of the basin, with suitable scour protection and headworks.

Infiltration basins can be designed as single units where the surface water inflow is unpolluted, or regular maintenance ensures that the infiltration performance is not affected by siltation. Otherwise, it is recommended that an inlet basin is constructed upstream of the main infiltration basin. The inlet basin should be sized to hold the first flush of polluted flow. The design of inlet basins is discussed under *Detention basins.*

The design of the main infiltration basin should take account of the following:

♦ is infiltration an acceptable method of surface water disposal at the site

♦ for storms with short recurrence intervals (under two years), half of the total storage volume should be available within 24 hours of a storm. This prevents waterlogging and keeps the grass cover in good condition. In extreme storms it will take longer to empty an infiltration basin

♦ the soil infiltration rate should be determined at the infiltration basin location. Refer to the section on *Soakaways and infiltration trenches* for details

♦ a site investigation should be carried out to determine whether or not the soil is suitable for infiltration drainage. This is particularly important on sites where there is filled ground, as the frequent discharge of additional waters may change the soil characteristics either chemically or structurally

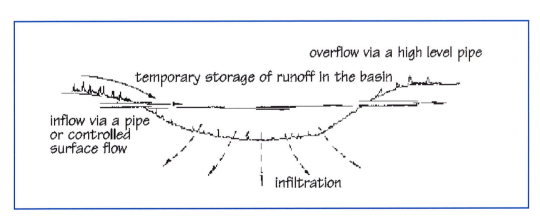

Cross-section through an infiltration basin, showing routes of inflow and outflow

- infiltration basins should not be constructed in ground where the water table reaches the bottom of the basin at any time of the year

- it is presently advised that infiltration systems should not be constructed within 5 m of roads or the foundations of buildings.

The inlet has been designed to prevent erosion. The basin has not been designed as a public amenity

The base of the basin should be flat, with side slopes of 1 in 4 or shallower (this is considered to be the steepest slope that can easily be negotiated by someone trying to exit the basin and that can be mowed with a ride-on mower). There should be a smooth transition between the base and sides of the infiltration basin.

For flows greater than the volume of the basin the following points should be considered:

- the overflow should be directed to a ditch or watercourse. Where this is not possible, it might be necessary to use adjacent land as informal storage (where surface flooding is permitted in such circumstances)

- an overflow to a ditch or watercourse should be provided to minimise the risk of the infiltration basin flooding in winter conditions

- where overflow is through an outfall pipe, the level of the pipe will need to be set to achieve minimum cover requirements

- the invert of the incoming discharge pipe should be the maximum level for providing the required design storage. This will provide emergency capacity between the pipe invert level and ground level.

During winter, the ground within the basin may freeze, reducing and temporarily preventing infiltration. This may cause the basin to fill, resulting in surface flooding. The degree of risk should be evaluated in the light of local weather records and of the available extra storage above design level in each case.

Construction

Construction and seeding of the infiltration basin should be carried out early in the construction phase of the development. This will allow the vegetation to become established before the basin comes into use.

The topsoil should be uniformly distributed and lightly compacted to a depth of 100 mm. Topsoil should not be placed while frozen or waterlogged, or when the sub-grade is excessively wet. The application of seed and fertiliser should be as uniform as possible.

The infiltration basin should be protected from traffic loading and surface water flows from the construction. It is recommended that temporary drainage systems are considered to carry runoff during the construction period. Compaction of the soil or deposition of large quantities of silt in an infiltration basin during construction will be detrimental to the basin's performance after completion.

To prevent the topsoil becoming dry while the vegetation becomes established, it might be necessary to irrigate the infiltration basin.

Safety

In infiltration basins that will contain a temporary pool of water after storms, a safety review should be carried out. If a barrier of some kind is required then barrier planting should be considered.

This provides amenity value in terms of appearance and provision of wildlife habitat. If the basin is next to a road, a vehicle barrier may be required. This could be formed by an earth bund which can then be planted.

At infiltration basins used for a secondary purpose, notices should be erected at the site. In conjunction with education of the local residents, such measures should emphasise that the basin is primarily a drainage device and should inform people how to use it safely.

Removal of material deposited in the inlet basin or on the base of the main infiltration basin should be considered. The accumulation of pollution may present little health hazard where inflows to the basin have occurred from roof surfaces or normal trafficked areas.

Operation and maintenance

Maintenance is limited to the surface of the infiltration basin. Regular grass cutting should be undertaken, and the grassed surface kept clear of leaves, silt and other debris. The intervals between mowing will depend on the local landscaping standards, and whether the basin has a secondary use, for example as a sports pitch. If barrier planting is used, this should be maintained in the same way as the local landscaping.

It is advantageous to scarify the soil regularly, to break up silt deposits and prevent over-compaction.

If the infiltration performance of the basin deteriorates, it might be necessary to remove and replace the grass and topsoil.

Amenity
Infiltration basins offer many opportunities to provide amenity value. If a basin is likely to remain dry for long periods of time, it can be used for a secondary purpose, such as a sports pitch or play area. If it is to be used for a secondary purpose, over-compaction of the soil should be avoided, and therefore use as a car park, for example, is not recommended.

Careful choice of indigenous plant species and grass types can be used to introduce local wild plants and flowers. This provides visual interest and could improve the habitat for local wildlife.

Detention basins

Detention basins are vegetated depressions. They are formed below the surrounding ground, and are dry except during and immediately following storm events. The basins provide storage that not only attenuates the flow, but also permits settlement of coarse silts. Detention basins only provide flood storage to attenuate flows. Extending the detention times improves water quality by permitting the settlement of coarse silts.

Design

During storm events, surface water runoff is routed through the extended detention basin. The outlet is restricted so that the basin fills with runoff. The control structure at the outlet is designed to release the retained water slowly, thereby providing time for suspended solids to settle out and for the flow peak to attenuate.

Their treatment efficiency is improved by an increase in detention times, but this will only cater for coarse particles. Finer sediments and dissolved contaminants require much longer detention times (see *Retention ponds*). More details on the design of detention basins are provided in *Design of flood storage reservoirs* (CIRIA, 1993). For water quality criteria, the detention basin should be sized to attenuate the relevant flood volume.

For water quantity criteria, the basic extended detention basin should be sized so that the design treatment volume, Vt (see *Selecting SUDS – design considerations*), can be fully contained. The outlet works should be designed so the basin empties over about 24 hours.

The maximum depth of water in the basin should not exceed 3 m at any time.

High sediment loads should be removed upstream, preferably at source or treated by a different SUDS device before the flow enters the detention basin. If this is not possible a settling basin can be provided at the inlet to the basin. This could consist of a separate basin or formed by building an earthen berm, stone/rock-filled gabion or riprap wall across the upstream portion of the main basin. The plan area should be between 10 per cent and 25 per cent of the total basin area.

A dry weather flow channel under construction

Inlets, outlets and overflows

The engineer can choose from various options for inlets, outlets and overflows. These are key control features and must be designed to suit the design criteria. If a control structure fails or is incorrectly designed, it can affect the performance of the whole drainage system.

Detailed advice on the design of inlet, outlet and overflow structures is given in *Design of flood storage reservoirs* (CIRIA, 1993).

Design criteria include the visual appearance of the controls, maintenance issues and hydraulic performance over a range of flow conditions.

A channel should be provided for dry weather flows. Other design considerations are generic to all basins and ponds and include:

- the basin volume can be increased to incorporate additional flood control detention storage. By using a multi-stage outlet, flows in excess of the treatment volume can be regulated to meet peak flow requirements

- the maximum side slope should be designed to meet safety and maintenance requirements

- energy dissipation and protection should be provided at the inlet to reduce erosion

- an overflow should be provided to deal with large storms and to ensure that a minimum 0.5 m freeboard is maintained in the basin

- slope protection might be needed during the construction and operation of the basin.

An inlet basin is a small impoundment located at the upstream end of the basin. It should be designed to capture the coarse sediments in the first flush of a storm. Flow from the inlet basin to the main basin should be arranged so that settled solids are not resuspended and floating litter is not washed downstream.

Maintenance will need to be more frequent in this area, but this should reduce the need to remove sediment from the main basin.

Construction

The following considerations in the construction of detention basins are common to all basins and ponds.

The bottom and side slopes of the basin should be carefully prepared to ensure that they are structurally sound, level and true. The preparation should also ensure that the basin will satisfactorily retain the surface water runoff without significant erosion damage. A liner or membrane may be used if infiltration has to be controlled.

The soils used to finish the side slopes and base of the basin need to be suitably fertile, porous and of sufficient depth to ensure healthy vegetation growth.

The landscape design should specify appropriate grass species (to give a dense sward) and plants that will grow well on the site and in the local soils. The choice of species must take into account the fact that the vegetation will be subject to periodic inundation and water flow.

The phasing of the construction should take into consideration the drainage needs during building and the subsequent performance of the basin.

Extended detention basins can be easy to access and maintain, but should also be designed to fit in with the surrounding landscape

Safety

Detention basins are normally dry, but safety should be considered for both wet and dry conditions.

Potential problems arising during the filling of the pond should be assessed. Shallow side slopes and easy access enable people to leave the area as it slowly floods.

A safety review should be carried out and, if necessary, a barrier provided. Barrier planting is an alternative to traditional fencing that provides greater value as a visual amenity and wildlife habitat. It is used extensively in Scandinavia.

Operation and maintenance

There should be adequate vehicular access to the main basin, inlet and outlet structures, settling pond and the dry weather channel, so that sediment can be removed during maintenance.

Maintenance requirements depend primarily on the nature of the landscaping employed. If planted with low-growing ground cover and shrubbery, twice-yearly inspection and repair of eroded and damaged areas should be sufficient.

Inlet and outlet structures should be inspected at least twice a year, and after large storms, for debris and erosion. Remedial action should be taken as necessary.

Sediment accumulations should be removed when necessary, taking appropriate measures to ensure the extracted material is disposed of properly and safely. Typically, sediment removal may be needed every seven to ten years, but periods of up to 25 years have also been estimated. Care should be taken to avoid damaging any liner.

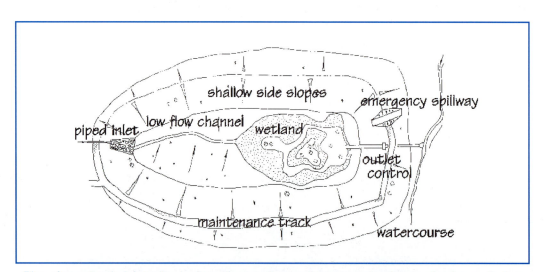

Plan of an extended detention basin, with a small area of permanant water as a landscape feature. Upstream source control has reduced the requirement for a silt trap at the inlet

Amenity

Detention basins can be designed for amenity as well as treatment and attenuation. The use of a variety of local plant species will provide wildlife habitats and improve the appearance of the basin. A permanent pool may be included within the basin.

The approach to designing basins for wildlife amenity is discussed more fully in the *Wetlands* section.

The inlet and outlet structures in an extended detention basin should be carefully designed to blend in with the surrounding landscape. It is important to remember that they will be visible during the long periods that the basin is dry or has a low water level. Control structures that incorporate gabion walls should include a settlement area to catch any solids washed out of the walls. Crushed concrete should be avoided as fill for gabion walls.

An outlet structure in Dunfermline

Retention ponds

Retention ponds are permanently wet ponds with rooted wetland and aquatic vegetation – mainly around the edge. The retention time of several days gives better settlement conditions than offered by extended detention ponds and provides a degree of biological treatment.

Design

The wetland and aquatic planting around the perimeter and across the width of a retention pond provides biological treatment of biodegradable pollutants and settlement of solids. Retention ponds are used as quality treatment facilities where extended treatment of the runoff is required. Some flood storage is also available, but it might be necessary to divert the less polluted large flood around the pond, to avoid inundating the peripheral vegetation.

The permanent pool of open water provides a relatively deep, still volume of water, in which suspended particulate contaminants can settle out. The vegetation:

💧 helps reduce the formation of algal mats

💧 enhances the visual and amenity value of the ponds

💧 provides a wildlife habitat

💧 slows down flows, increasing settlement

💧 aids treatment.

The basic retention pond permanent pool volume should be sized to contain four times the design treatment volume V_t (see *Selecting SUDS – design considerations*). This volume should provide a residual pond retention time of approximately 14 to 21 days during the wettest months. As well as allowing time for biological treatment to occur, it also improves the degree of suspended particulate settlement and ultimate removal.

The average depth of water in the permanent pool should be between 1 m and 2 m, with the maximum water depth limited to about 3 m. The maximum pond side slope should be limited to 1 in 4 to meet safety and maintenance requirements.

Open water in retention ponds should occupy 50-75 per cent of the permanent pond surface area. The remaining area should be used to create a shallow bench about 0.5 m deep. This bench is provided around the perimeter of the pond and should be at least 3 m wide. It should be fully planted with emergent aquatic vegetation selected to suit local climatic, soil and water depth factors.

The design considerations common to all ponds and wetlands are discussed in the section on *Detention basins*.

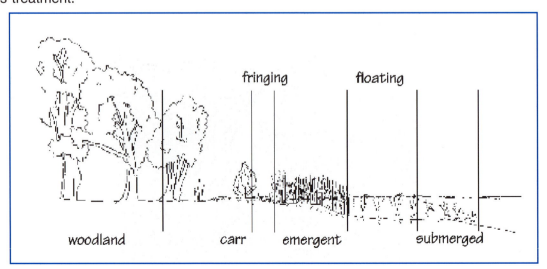

Typical vegetation sequence across a retention pond

The following additional considerations should be made for the design of retention ponds:

- the permanent pool volume is provided below the outlet level

- short-circuiting of flows should be minimised by using a length-to-width ratio of at least 3:1, with the inlet and outlets at opposite ends. Windbreaks may be needed to reduce the influence of the wind on flow patterns. **Baffles** can also extend the flow path

- the additional detention storage provided for flood control should be limited to 2 m above the permanent pool level to avoid damage to the vegetation in the pond

- the outlet works should provide a smooth stage discharge relationship for discharge of storm flows from the pond. This may be achieved, for example, with a V-notch weir transitioning into a sharp crested horizontal weir. Details on the design of different inlet and outlet control structures are provided in *Design of flood storage reservoirs* (CIRIA, 1993)

- if no detention storage for peak flow control is to be added above the permanent pool level, the outlet works may be relatively simple.

Construction

The general construction aspects of ponds and wetlands are discussed in *Detention basins*. As retention ponds rely on vegetation to enhance the treatment effect, the establishment period should be included in the construction programme.

> **Baffles:** islands, promontories and submerged shoals can prevent the runoff from flowing directly from the inlet to the outlet. They also provide visual interest and variation in habitat.

Retention pond

Safety

The general safety aspects of ponds and wetlands are discussed in *Detention basins*.

Retention ponds have permanent open water of significant depth. The side slopes should be gentle to allow easy exit. If shallow margins cannot be provided, scramble rocks can make it easier to get out of the pond.

If a safety review considers it necessary, the edge could be fully planted with aquatic and densely planted waterside vegetation. Paths through this barrier planting could provide controlled access to the pond, and should be carefully designed with the public in mind.

Amenity

When properly established, retention ponds should be permanent water facilities with well-maintained, vegetated margins and water surfaces. As such, they should be visually pleasing features that can be beneficially incorporated within the development landscaping. The open water and aquatic and marginal vegetation can provide a variety of wildlife habitats.

The water stored in attenuation ponds, retention ponds and wetlands can be extracted for reuse. The use of water as a resource in this way is becoming more widespread as the cost of providing water continues to rise.

In addition to providing opportunities for wildlife and birds, permanent pools can be used for recreation. Fishing, boating and other watersports such as windsurfing and water-skiing are possible on ponds with permanent water. Careful choice of local plant species and grass types can be used to provide aesthetic value, and could improve the habitat for local wildlife. The principles of designing ponds and vegetation to provide wildlife habitats are discussed in the *Wetlands* section.

Operation and maintenance

Adequate maintenance access is needed to the pond and inlet and outlet structures. The vegetation around the edge should be inspected quarterly for nuisance plants during the first two years of establishment.

Inlet and outlet structures should be inspected twice a year and after large storms for debris and erosion, with remedial action taken as necessary.

Sediment accumulations should be removed, typically once every seven to ten years, although well-designed source control may extend this to 25 years. All the necessary measures should be taken to ensure the proper and safe disposal of the dredged material. Precautions should also be taken to avoid damaging any impermeable liner.

Wetlands

Wetlands comprise relatively shallow ponds and marshland areas covered almost entirely in aquatic vegetation. Wetland vegetation is well suited for the biological treatment and removal of dissolved contaminants and nutrients, and the use of wetlands for water and wastewater treatment is well documented.

Design

The basic wetland permanent pool volume should be sized to contain three times the design treatment volume, V_t (see *Selecting SUDS – design considerations*). This size of permanent pool volume should provide a residual wetland retention time of up to 14 days during the wettest months. This allows time for biological treatment to occur and improves the degree of suspended particulate settlement or removal. It is important to ensure that there is sufficient **baseflow** to keep the wetland operating in dry periods.

> **Baseflow:** the flow required in dry weather to compensate for water losses through evaporation, infiltration and plant uptake.

Wetlands are ecosystems, and are most successful when they provide a wide range of habitats for plants and wildlife. For this reason, wetlands should be designed as pond mosaics or linked complexes, rather than isolated water bodies. For variety, deep and shallow standing water should be provided, with running water at inlets and outlets, if possible. Water depth in wetlands should vary from less than 0.6 m at the edges to a maximum water depth of 3 m or more. Water deeper than 3 m inhibits rooted plant growth, thus providing areas of open water. However, deep water can stratify, leading to a layer of foul water at the bottom of the wetland. In this case, aeration or artificial mixing could be considered to avoid problems of odour or low oxygen content. Temporary detention storage should be limited to 2 m to prevent damage to vegetation.

Shorelines can vary from deep and overhanging to shallow beaches, if ground conditions permit. In larger wetlands, natural islands or floating rafts help segregate animal and plant communities, and provide visual interest. Both safety and the provision of wildlife habitat should be considered when deciding the pond profile.

Shallow side slopes (eg 1 in 4) should be provided where needed for safety and maintenance. Stepped or steeply sloping banks help to stop the spread of invasive emergent plant species. Shallow sloping spits of land can be incorporated into the wetland banks. These break up the edge into a series of linked pools, and the shallow slopes will encourage access by wildlife such as aquatic mammals, amphibians and reptiles.

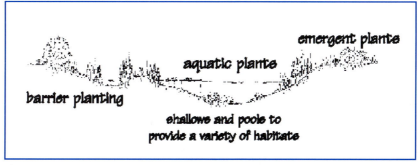

Cross-section of a wetland

Open water in wetlands should occupy no more than a quarter of the wetland surface area. The remaining area should comprise shallows up to a maximum 0.5 m deep. The shallows should be fully planted with emergent aquatic vegetation, selected to suit the local climate, soil and water depths. Wetlands can provide habitats ranging from open water, through littoral with submerged and emergent plants, reedbed and marsh grasses, carr willow and alder scrub, to wet grassland suitable for occasional or seasonal grazing. Guidance on how to provide appropriate habitats for particular plant and animal species can be obtained from SEPA. Other sources of information include publications such as *Wetlands, industry and wildlife* (Wildfowl and Wetland Trust, 1994), *The new river and wildlife handbook* (RSPB, NRA & RSNC, 1994) and *Water level requirements of wetland plants and animals* (English Nature, 1997).

Reference should also be made to the common design aspects of ponds and wetlands discussed in *Detention basins and Retention ponds*, and to the *Review of the design and management of constructed wetlands* (CIRIA, 1997).

Construction

The general construction aspects of ponds and wetlands are discussed in *Detention basins*.

If an impermeable liner is used, care should be taken to ensure that it is not damaged during construction.

Safety

The general safety aspects of ponds and wetlands are discussed in *Detention basins*.

Barrier planting should be used round the margins of the wetland, particularly near deep water. This planting should prevent access to the relatively small areas of open water within the wetland. Peripheral planting also reduces the disturbance to bird and animal life.

A wetland under construction

Operation and maintenance

General aspects of the operation and maintenance of wetlands are discussed in *Detention basins* and *Retention ponds.*

To maintain the diversity and effectiveness of a wetland in the long term it is important to agree an **environmental management plan** with relevant bodies. This should include a management and maintenance programme to ensure that the wetland is successfully established in the first few years, and then continues to operate as an effective drainage device.

> **Environmental management plan:** a management agreement for an area or project which is set up to make sure the declared management objectives for the area or project are met. EMPs are often undertaken as part of an environmental impact assessment and are set out in several stages with responsibilities clearly set down and environmental monitoring in place to show compliance with the plan.

Inspection for sediment and debris accumulation should be carried out annually. Inlets and outlets should be inspected more frequently, especially after large storms. If sediment is not being removed upstream, an inlet basin will ease the removal of deposited solids from the wetland. This should be regularly desilted, typically every four to five years. Capturing the silt in an inlet basin will reduce the need to dredge wetlands to once every 25 years or less.

Aquatic vegetation within the wetland should be cut back after flowering, and thinned when necessary, typically every seven to ten years. Measures should be taken to ensure the proper and safe disposal of the extracted material. Care should also be taken to avoid damaging any impermeable liner present.

Some control over unwanted algal growth can be obtained in open water areas of the wetland using barley or straw bales.

Peripheral and barrier planting should be maintained in line with local landscaping standards.

> **Amenity**
> When fully established, wetlands can be facilities that are attractive and have considerable amenity value. Their incorporation into the general landscaping of the development should be beneficial.
>
> Ponds and wetlands provide the greatest opportunity to improve habitats for mammals, fish, birds and reptiles. If design is undertaken with wildlife habitat in mind, the resulting wetland will be an attractive and educational feature, with a variety of plant and wildlife species making it their home.

A Maintenance framework

Framework for a maintenance agreement for new developments

AGREEMENT UNDER SECTION 7 OF THE SEWERAGE (SCOTLAND) ACT 1968

This is a framework for an agreement between the Local Authority (as the roads authority referred to in the Roads (Scotland) Act 1984) and the Water Authority (as the drainage authority referred to in the Sewerage (Scotland) Act 1968). This agreement will be reviewed two years after the publication date of "Sustainable urban drainage systems – design manual for Scotland and Northern Ireland".

This agreement relates only to the situation where it is proposed that the drainage of surface water from adopted roads and the curtilage water from premises be directed through a shared system designed in accordance with the manual.

The maintenance of sections of a drainage system upstream of the point of connection to the shared system will continue to be the responsibility of the relevant authority.

Section 1 relates to the situation where SUDS are not required.

Section 2 relates to the position where SUDS are necessary.

Section 3 relates to the future management responsibilities.

Section 1 – Agreement where SUDS are not required

From shared surface water systems where SUDS are not considered necessary by the Scottish Environment Protection Agency (SEPA), the Water Authority will own and maintain the collector sewers and associated manholes from the point where the system becomes shared (i.e. where the tails of road gullies connect to the sewer) to the point of discharge.

Entry into the shared sewer for road water will be via a trapped gully and, where considered necessary by the Water Authority, approved hydrocarbon separators.

Maintenance of the gullies and separators shall be the responsibility of the Local Authority.

Where the quality of surface water at the point of discharge becomes an issue with SEPA, it shall be dealt with in accordance with Section 3 of this Agreement.

19

Section 2 – Agreement where SUDS are required

In any case where SUDS are required by SEPA as part of the shared surface water drainage system, the allocation of maintenance responsibility shall be as follows:-

- above-ground works such as grass swales, retention ponds, detention ponds, etc shall be taken over and maintained by the Local Authority

- below-ground structures, such as piped systems (including perforated pipes and surrounding material), soakaways, catchpits, filter drains etc will be owned and maintained by the Water Authority.

The Water Authority will also be responsible for the discharge into watercourses where applicable.

Section 3 – Future management

In the event that SEPA considers that the receiving watercourse is deteriorating because of the quality of the discharge from the shared system, the matter will be considered by a regional group consisting of SEPA, the Local Authority and the Water Authority who will seek to agree what, if any, remedial measures are appropriate. The costs of such additional work will be apportioned in a ratio equivalent to the degree of contribution to the cause of deterioration. If agreement on a way forward cannot be reached then the issue will be referred to the national Working Party (SUDSWP) who will attempt to offer a resolution.

While this *framework for a maintenance agreement for new developments* will apply in most developments the local authority or water authority reserves the right to require a Site Specific Agreement involving third parties where a development requires major sustainable urban drainage systems and/or flood attenuation measures.

B Information checklist

The following checklist sets out the information required to progress drainage design to the preliminary design level required for a planning application. Calculations, plans and cross-sections of the drainage system should be submitted, along with site layout drawings and landscaping drawings and maintenance schedules. This has been drawn up for Scotland. The consultees will need to be amended for Northern Ireland.

Description	Details for the particular project	Consultees and sources of information
Existing topography		Site inspections, local authority plans
Details of receiving sewer/ watercourse/aquifer		Water authority, SEPA, local authority
Quantity/discharge design criteria		Water authority, SEPA, local authority
Quality design criteria, level of treatment		Water authority, SEPA, local authority
Rainfall data (preferably recorded)		Met Office, site observations
Hydrology of catchment (including greenfield runoff)		Site observations
Soil type and infiltration potential		Site tests
Environmentally sensitive areas		SEPA, local authority, Scottish Natural Heritage
Development type, land use		Client, engineer, planner and regulator
Size of entire catchment, likely impermeable areas		Client, engineer, planner and landscape architect
Availability and cost of land		Client and planner
Sub-catchment types within development		Client, engineer, planner and regulator
Proposed topography		Client, engineer, planner, SEPA, local authority, landscape architect
Amenity provision		Local authority, landscape architect, local residents and pressure groups
Ecology, wildlife habitat provision		SEPA, wildlife protection groups, Scottish Natural Heritage
Health and safety considerations		All affected parties

☐ Existing data to be collected

☐ Design and planning criteria to be decided

C Worked design examples

Determining the design treatment volume

To treat just the polluted runoff, the early part of major storms need to be captured. Some basic criteria are set out in this manual, but these do not take into account site-specific conditions and so tend to be conservative. In an effort to model the situation in more detail, work has been carried out to determine the treatment volumes that capture 75-90 per cent of the storms in a year. Larger storms can be diverted around treatment facilities, with only the initial runoff being treated. The following examples describe how to:

● use standard data and the Wallingford Procedure to determine a **design treatment volume V_t** for a particular site

● determine a site-specific **design treatment volume V_t** using the STORM computer model and recorded rainfall data.

Examples outlining the use of the Wallingford Procedure

The **Wallingford Procedure** is a set of guidelines widely used in the UK and overseas for the design and analysis of urban drainage systems. Volume 3 contains a series of standard maps covering the United Kingdom, which show the geographical distribution of rainfall depths (M5-60 minutes) and winter rain acceptance potential (WRAP).

If detailed rainfall data for a particular site is not available, the Wallingford Procedure maps can be used to obtain the unit design treatment volume **V_t** as follows.

1. Establish with reasonable accuracy the location of the development site in question.

2. Plot the location on both the M5-60 rainfall map and the WRAP map and determine the M5-60 rainfall depth "D" (in millimetres) and the value of the soil index (SOIL) from the WRAP soil classification (1, 2, 3, 4 or 5).

3. Use the following equation to calculate the treatment volume:

    V_t *(m³/ha)* = 9•D(SOIL/2 + (1-SOIL/2)•I)
    (equation for Vt)

    where **I** is the impervious fraction of the area (30% impervious ✂ I = 0.3)

    D is the M5-60 rainfall depth from the Volume 3 plans, and

    For the Dunfermline development site:

    WRAP soil classification is 4, giving a SOIL of 0.45
    D is 13.4 mm.

    V_t *(m³/ha)* = 9•13.4(0.45/2 + (1-(0.45/2))•I)
    = 120.6•(0.225+0.775•I)
    V_t *(m³/ha)* = 27 + 94•I

    In comparison, a site near Ballachulish with M5-60 of 19mm, WRAP 5 and SOIL = 0.5:

    V_t *(m³/ha)* = 9•D(SOIL/2 + (1-SOIL/2)•I)
    V_t *(m³/ha)* = 9•19.0(0. 5/2 + (1-(0.5/2))•I)
    = 171.0•(0. 25+0.75•I)

    V_t *(m³/ha)* = 43 + 128•I

For a development site of 45 per cent impermeable area and a detention basin depth of 2 m, the treatment volume and land take for the two sites would be:

Dunfermline: 69.2 m³/ha   (0.35% of the site)
Ballachulish: 100.5 m³/ha   (1.0% of the site)

A new development near Ballachulish would require larger extended detention basins than an identical development at Dunfermline. This is as expected, as both the M5-60 storm and the average annual rainfall are greater on the west side of Scotland than at Dunfermline. The lower infiltration potential also increases the runoff.

For general use, it is recommended that the Wallingford Procedure be used to determine the design treatment volume for a development site.

The equation for V_t used in this analysis was developed from hourly rainfall data at Dunfermline over a four-year data collection period. They are based on a treatment volume that captures the runoff from 90 per cent of storms occurring in a one-year period.

To check that this equation was applicable across the UK, an analysis was undertaken to compare the runoff from recorded annual timeseries events in Dunfermline, Edinburgh, Belfast and south-west England and the treatment volume calculated using the method described above.

The Modified Rational Method and a standard set of assumptions were used to calculate the runoff from all the timeseries events. The average runoff was calculated, and compared against the treatment volume arrived at using the Wallingford Procedure calculation above.

A correlation between V_t for each site calculated from the Wallingford Procedure and the annual average runoff was obtained. This indicated that the Wallingford Procedure equation was suitable for the calculation of treatment volume across the UK.

The concepts of treatment volume and first flush of pollution are understood. However, there is limited research data available to explore and quantify the link between rainfall, runoff, first flush and required treatment volume for quality. The equation developed above indicates current best practice but would benefit from further research.

Example outlining the use of the STORM computer model

STORM is a relatively simple model used for computerised assessment of detention basin performance. It is based on equations used in the *California stormwater best practice management practice handbook.* Using site rainfall data and a series of runoff coefficients representing different degrees of development, STORM calculates a corresponding sequence of runoff values. The runoff is then routed through a detention basin, with a discharge rate determined such that the full basin would drain over a period of 15-24 hours. This 24-hour period has been selected as the detention time required to achieve effective settlement of an acceptable proportion of pollutants in the basin.

During a study conducted for a large development site to the east of Dunfermline, four consecutive years of hourly rainfall data were analysed using the STORM model. The results are shown in the figure below. These show that, for all levels of development, the percent capture of annual rainfall increases with treatment volume, with an optimum capture level lying at the knee of the curve. A 90 per cent capture level was found to provide an optimum compromise between pollutant capture and treatment volume. At this level, most small storms, and the first flush components of larger storms, are captured and treated.

The intersection points on the 90 per cent capture line on the figure show two extremes.

For a fully pervious sub-catchment located within development areas where runoff should be treated, 90 per cent of the annual storms can be captured and treated by capturing the first 2.5 mm of runoff. However, if an area is undeveloped and fully pervious, there is no need to treat the runoff and no storm detention is required. If an undeveloped area drains into the same treatment facility as a developed area, then allowance will have to be made for the volume of runoff, based on this 2.5 mm level.

For a 100 per cent impervious, developed site, runoff from 90 per cent of the annual storms can be captured and treated by capturing the first 11.5 mm of runoff.

The table shows the relationship between the 90 per cent capture and ideal design treatment volume for a range of impermeable areas. This data has been read from the curves developed for the Dunfermline site.

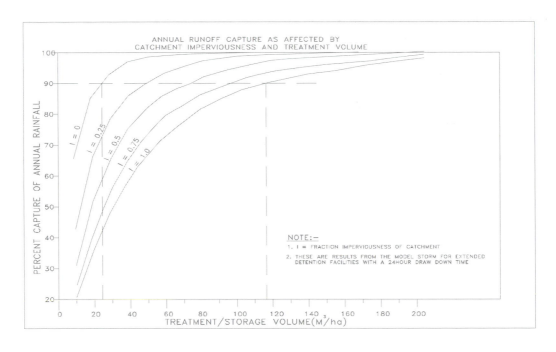

Impervious area (%)	Volume (m³/ha)
0	25
10	34
20	43
30	52
40	61
50	70
60	79
70	88
80	97
90	106
100	115

From this data, an equation defining the relationship between impervious area and treatment/storage volume can be developed to describe the unit treatment volume V_t at the Dunfermline site:

V_t *(m³/ha)* = 25 + 90•I

where **I** is the average impervious fraction of the area (30% impermeable area – I = 0.3).

The total design treatment volume required for the treatment facility is calculated by:

Total design treatment volume = V_t x Total catchment area *(ha)*

This corresponds well with the equation obtained from the less detailed Wallingford Procedure analysis of rainfall data for the same site, which yielded a value of V_t *(m³/ha)* = 27 + 94•I

Note that the use of site-specific data gives a smaller volume V_t than the more conservative procedure using the Wallingford Procedure.

Example of the design of a filter strip and swale

This example describes the process of designing conveyance devices using the Manning equation. The process is iterative, and several design passes will be made before the optimum design is reached. For clarity, this example only contains the calculations for the final iteration.

Description	Details for the particular project	Consultees and sources of information
Existing topography	Generally flat, with a slight slope towards a burn at the eastern side	Site inspections, local authority plans
Details of receiving sewer/ watercourse/aquifer	The stream is a sensitive watercourse	Water authority, SEPA, local authority
Quantity/discharge design criteria	Drainage devices should contain a 20-year return period storm	Water authority, SEPA, local authority
Quality design criteria, level of treatment	Sports field: one level of treatment; car park: two levels of treatment	Water authority, SEPA, local authority
Rainfall data (preferably recorded)	None available	Met Office, site observations
Hydrology of catchment	Not available	Site observations
Soil type and infiltration potential	Unknown	Site tests
Environmentally sensitive areas	None	SEPA, local authority, Scottish Natural Heritage
Development type, land use	1 ha recreational site, comprising sports field, car park & changing room	Client, engineer, planner and regulator
Size of entire catchment, likely impermeable areas	1 ha total area. Sports field: 0.5ha; car park and changing room: 0.5ha	Client, engineer, planner and landscape architect
Availability and cost of land	Already negotiated	Client and planner
Sub-catchment types within development	Recreational/residential only	Client, engineer, planner and regulator
Proposed topography	As existing. Sports field to be graded	Client, engineer, planner, SEPA, local authority, landscape architect
Amenity provision	None	Local authority, landscape architect, local residents and pressure groups
Ecology, wildlife habitat provision	None required	SEPA, wildlife protection groups, Scottish Natural Heritage
Health and safety considerations	No specific requirements	All affected parties

Other design considerations

The sports field maintenance includes regular mowing to maintain grass length. For this reason, the preferred drainage option is a grassed swale, the maintenance of which can be easily integrated into existing maintenance procedures for the site.

The car park requires a second level of treatment, so a filter strip will be integrated with the swale around the edges of the car parking area.

Design of filter strip

Car park and changing room area	=	0.5 ha
Time of entry into filter strip	=	5 minutes
Critical 20-year rainfall intensity	=	98 mm/h

100% impervious area $\therefore Q_{max}$ = 100% x 98 mm/h x 0.5 ha = 136 l/s

Grass length = 50 to 150 mm. With negligible submergence, can assume Manning's "n" = 0.25.

Width available for filter strip	=	50 m
Slope of filter strip	=	approximately 2%.

Use Manning's equation to determine depth of flow:

$Q = AR^{2/3}S^{1/2}/n$ where

	A	=	cross-sectional area of flow (m²)
		=	width x depth of flow
	R	=	hydraulic radius = A/P (m)
	P	=	wetted perimeter (m)
	S	=	ground slope in direction of flow (m/m)
	n	=	Manning's roughness coefficient
$\therefore$ depth of flow		=	40 mm

(This confirms assumptions about negligible submergence and Manning's "n" are appropriate.)
Corresponding velocity of flow = 0.1 m/s, so this design is adequate in terms of treatment requirements. Area of land take depends on configuration of car park.

Design of swale

Total catchment area to outlet of swale	=	1 ha
Length of swale	=	250 m
Gradient of swale	=	1.5%
Side slopes	=	1 in 5
Width of base	=	1 m

Design for conveyance of 20-year, 60 min storm:
I_{max} = 75 mm/h
50% impervious, $\therefore Q_{max}$ = 0.5 x 75 mm/h x 1.0 ha = 104 l/s

Again, using iteration and Manning's formula:
For a Manning's "n" of 0.25, the depth of flow would be 280 mm, representing complete submergence of the grass. Manning's "n" would therefore be reduced in accordance with the relationship between 'n' and depth of flow presented in *Filter strips*.

By iteration:	Manning's "n"	=	0.06
	Depth of flow	=	140 mm
	Flow velocity	=	0.4 m/s

Design for treatment of one-year, 60 min storm:
$I_{average}$ = 15 mm/h
$\therefore Q_{max}$ = 0.5 x 15 mm/h x 1.0 ha = 21 l/s

By iteration:	N	=	0.14
	Depth of flow	=	95 mm (design criteria require <0.1 m)
	Velocity of flow	=	0.15 m/s (design criteria require <0.3 m/s)

All parameters satisfy requirements for design of swales for water quality treatment. Detailed design, including suitable outlet configuration and protection can now be undertaken. If the total swale depth is 300 mm, the land take is 10 per cent of the site, although this would included land for road verges, open space etc.

Example of the procedure for designing permeable pavements

The design of permeable pavements is generally undertaken in accordance with manufacturers' literature, once an appropriate surfacing material has been selected. This example identifies the criteria that a designer might consider when designing and selecting permeable paving materials.

Design considerations
What is the purpose of the pavement?

♦ to infiltrate water into the sub-grade for disposal or to maintain soil moisture content

♦ to attenuate surface water runoff within the sub-base for flow control

♦ to attenuate surface water runoff within the sub-base for reuse

♦ to provide a surface protected by vegetation to prevent erosion

♦ to provide treatment to surface water runoff before disposal

♦ to remove or reduce costs of positive drainage for the site.

What surface finish is required?

♦ smooth finishes for medium and heavy traffic loading, trolleys, wheelchairs, footpaths – choose tesselating permeable or porous concrete blocks, porous macadam

♦ rough finishes for light traffic loads (eg car parks), green areas or landscaping reasons – choose open-cell concrete blocks, concrete grass paviors or gravel.

What is the infiltration rate through the pavement surface and into the sub-base?

♦ permeable tesselating concrete block surfaces   4500 mm/h

♦ porous macadam   10 000 mm/h

♦ concrete grass paviors (depending on % open area)   >50 mm/h

♦ gravel   >5000 mm/h

What type of sub-base should be used? This depends on:

♦ the voids ratio required to provide the attenuation volume

♦ the strength requirements for the loading conditions.

Can surface water runoff be allowed to infiltrate into the sub-grade? This depends on whether:

♦ the strength of the sub-grade will decrease with frequent wetting over time

♦ the sub-grade contains materials which decompose or change volume

♦ there is a likelihood that water in the sub-grade will flow towards building or road foundations less than 5 m away

♦ the surface water runoff may be contaminated with pollutants that should not enter the soil

♦ the sub-grade contains pollutants that might be mobilised by infiltration and enter the groundwater.

What is the infiltration rate of surface water runoff into the sub-grade?

♦ This should be determined by site tests. Refer to the section on *Design of soakaways and infiltration trenches* and BRE Digest 365.

What land take is required?

♦ As the pavement has a dual purpose, no additional land is required for the drainage system.

Maintenance considerations

The choice of permeable paving type may depend on the maintenance requirements of the pavement surface.

How often will the pavement be swept?

◆ silt and debris adversely affect the infiltration capabilities of all permeable pavements

◆ porous asphalt and concrete blocks with fine surface voids are likely to block fastest.

Is there provision for grass cutting and weed control?

◆ gravel, open-cell concrete blocks and concrete grass paviors will need maintaining

◆ porous asphalt and tesselating concrete blocks with fine surface voids do not generally require either grass cutting or weed control.

What are the long-term maintenance provisions to reinstate the free-draining characteristics of the surface?

◆ gravel and open-cell concrete blocks can be jetted and blockages removed

◆ the voids in concrete grass paviors can be riddled

◆ tesselating concrete blocks and porous asphalt should be replaced completely

◆ if voids in the sub-base become blocked, the entire pavement should be dug up and reinstated, either with existing or new materials.

Example of the design of an infiltration trench

This example describes the process of designing infiltration devices using the processes described in BRE Digest 365 and CIRIA Report 156, *Infiltration drainage – manual of good practice.*

Description	Details for the particular project	Consultees and sources of information
Existing topography	Slight slope to rear of houses	Site inspections, local authority plans
Details of receiving sewer/ watercourse/aquifer	Groundwater is not protected, so infiltration is possible	Water authority, SEPA, local authority
Quantity/discharge design criteria	None	Water authority, SEPA, local authority
Quality design criteria, level of treatment	None	Water authority, SEPA, local authority
Rainfall data (preferably recorded)	Not available – use maps in Wallingford Procedure Vol 3	Met Office, site observations
Hydrology of catchment	Not available	Site observations
Soil type and infiltration potential	Site tests show soil infiltration 180 mm/h or 5×10^{-5} m/s to a depth of 2m below ground	Site tests
Environmentally sensitive areas	None	SEPA, local authority, Scottish Natural Heritage
Development type, land use	Part of a residential development in Nairn. Sub-catchment is five terraced houses	Client, engineer, planner and regulator
Size of entire catchment, likely impermeable areas	Roof area $5 \times 150m^2 = 750m^2$. Individual house $150m^2$	Client, engineer, planner and landscape architect
Availability and cost of land	Already negotiated	Client and planner
Sub-catchment types within development	Residential only – house roofs requiring one level of treatment	Client, engineer, planner and regulator
Proposed topography	As existing	Client, engineer, planner, SEPA, local authority, landscape architect
Amenity provision	None in this sub-catchment	Local authority, landscape architect, local residents and pressure groups
Ecology, wildlife habitat provision	None in this sub-catchment	SEPA, wildlife protection groups, Scottish Natural Heritage
Health and safety considerations	None	All affected parties

Design of infiltration trench

Using BRE 365, sizing of an infiltration device is calculated by:

Inflow – Outflow = Storage

Inflow = Impermeable area x Total rainfall in ten-year return period storm (10y60 in this case)

Total rainfall, as calculated from BRE 365:
M5-60 rainfall ratio (r) = 0.23
M5-60 rainfall depth = 20 mm for Nairn
Z2 factor for Scotland and Northern Ireland

Duration (D)	Z1	M5-D	Z2	M10-D	Inflow from house
15 min	0.55	11 mm	1.19	13.1 mm	2.0 m³
30 min	0.74	12.8 mm	1.20	15.4 mm	2.3 m³
60 min	1.00	20 mm	1.19	23.8 mm	3.6 m³
120 min	1.31	26.2 mm	1.18	30.9 mm	4.6 m³
240 min	1.73	34.6 mm	1.18	40.8 mm	6.1 m³
360 min	2.04	40.8 mm	1.17	47.7 mm	7.2 m³

Outflow $\quad=\quad a_{s50}$ x soil infiltration rate x storm duration

$a_{s50} \quad=\quad$ surface area of trench sides to 50% effective depth
effective depth is depth below the invert of the incoming pipe
length of trench serving one house = 10 m

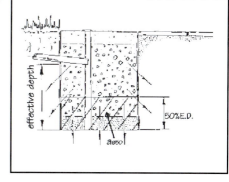

$$a_{s50} \quad = \quad 2 \times (10+W) \times (1.0 \times 0.5)$$
$$= \quad 10+W$$

Outflow $\quad = \quad (10+W) \times 0.180m/h \times$ duration (h)
Outflow $\quad = \quad 1.8D + 0.18DW$

Storage volume at 40% voids $\quad = \quad 1.0 \times W \times 0.4$
$$= \quad 4W$$

From equation: Inflow – Outflow = Storage:

Duration (D)	Inflow from house	W
15 min	2.0 m³	0.38 m
30 min	2.3 m³	0.34 m
60 min	3.6 m³	0.43 m
120 min	4.6 m³	0.23 m
240 min	6.1 m³	-ve
360 min	7.2 m³	-ve

From this calculation, an infiltration trench 10 m long x 0.43 m bucket width x 2 m deep will drain one house.

For the five-house sub-catchment, an infiltration trench 50 m long in the rear gardens is needed. If each house and garden is 300 m², land take is 1.4 per cent.

Example of the procedure for designing wetlands

This example identifies the criteria that might be considered when designing a wetland for treatment of surface water runoff.

Wetlands are complex ecosystems, constantly changing and reacting to their environment. They treat runoff by attenuation and the action of wetland vegetation. The volume of runoff stored in a wetland and the retention time can be calculated using basic hydraulic equations, as described in *Selecting SUDS*. The selection of vegetation, and provision of suitable habitats for plant and wildlife is a most important aspect of wetlands, and each site will be different.

Design considerations
What are the purposes of the wetland?
- to attenuate surface water runoff for flow and flood control

- to provide treatment to surface water runoff by attenuation and settlement

- to provide treatment to surface water runoff by biological action of plants and animals

- to provide additional or replacement wetland habitats for nature conservation

- to provide visual or recreational amenity features.

Environmental issues
How much land is available, and at what cost?
- can a wetland be developed without adversely affecting neighbouring land uses? For example, raising water levels can affect nearby crops

- wetlands can lead to increased evaporative losses – in estuarine areas this could lead to salination of the groundwater

- what habitats are sought? These can include open water, littoral with submerged and emergent plants, reedbed and marsh grasses, carr willow and alder scrub, or wet grassland suitable for occasional and seasonal grazing

- wetlands attract birds, which could become an air safety issue if a wetland is close to an airport or on a flightpath

- are all the potential uses compatible with each other? Is the wetland large enough to accept them all, or is spatial or temporal zoning required?

Other design issues
Is there a constant baseflow, or will the wetland be a seasonal feature?
- what is the range of flood flows and water levels? How can water levels be controlled?

- what retention time is needed?

- is there a need for aeration due to depth, for pH correction, fishery protection or odour control?

- what pollutants will be present in the surface water runoff? Will these require settlement areas, pH correction or floating booms or reed barriers to remove them?

- what are the soil or ground conditions? Will an impermeable liner be required to avoid excessive drying, or to protect the groundwater?

Maintenance considerations
Wetlands need regular maintenance, particularly sediment removal and plant management. It is important that an environmental management plan is agreed and implemented if wetlands are to remain effective drainage devices.

- in the early years of establishment, plant growth should be monitored every three months, and unwanted vegetation removed seasonally

- although a range of shorelines is recommended to maximise biodiversity, shallow shelves can be included to ease access for construction and maintenance

- oil booms or silt traps need to be accessible for regular maintenance.

Bibliography

BRE, 1991. *Soakaway design.* BRE Digest 365

CIRIA, 1987. *Design of reinforced grass waterways.* Report 116

CIRIA, 1993. *Design of flood storage reservoirs.* Book 14

CIRIA/Butterworths, 1990. *Use of vegetation in civil engineering*

CIRIA, 1992. *Scope for control of urban runoff.* Report 123

CIRIA, 1994. *Control of pollution from highway runoff.* Report 142

CIRIA, 1995. *Sediment management in urban drainage catchments.* Report 134

CIRIA, 1996. *Infiltration drainage – manual of good practice.* Report 156

CIRIA, 1997. *Design of containment systems for the prevention of water pollution from industrial incidents.* Report 164

CIRIA, 1997. *Review of the design and management of constructed wetlands.* Report 180

CIRIA, 1999. *The prevention of pollution from construction sites*

English Nature, 1997. *Water level requirements of wetland plants and animals*

Institute of Hydrology, 1999. *Flood estimation handbook*

Institute of Hydrology, 1975. *Flood studies report*

RSPB, NRA & RSNC, 1994. *The new rivers and wildlife handbook*

The Wildfowl and Wetlands Trust, 1994. *Wetlands, industry and wildlife*

SEPA, 1997. *Groundwater protection policy for Scotland.* Policy No 19

CIRIA, 1999. *Sustainable urban drainage – best practice.* Publication C523

Ven Te Chow, 1959. *Open channel hydraulics*

Urbanas, B and Stahre, P, 1983. *Stormwater best management practices and detention for water quality, drainage and CSO management.* Prentice Hall

Wilson, E M, 1987 *Engineering Hydrology*

Novotny, V and Olem, H, 1994. *Water quality: prevention, identification and management of diffuse pollution.* Chapman & Hall

Local Government Management Board, 1994. *Local Agenda 21 – A framework for local sustainability*

The Stationery Office, 1991. *Water Industry Act*

The Stationery Office, 1980. *Control of Pollution Act*

The Stationery Office, 1968. *Sewerage (Scotland) Act*

The Stationery Office, 1984. *Roads (Scotland) Act*

The Stationery Office, 1997. *Flood Prevention and Land Drainage (Scotland) Act*

The Stationery Office, 1997. *Town and Country Planning (Scotland) Act*

The Stationery Office, 1973. *Local Government Scotland Act*

The Stationery Office, 1974. *Local Government Scotland Act*

The Scottish Office, *NPPG7 Planning and flooding*

The Stationery Office, 1995. *Environment Act*

SEPA, *PPG3 Use and design of oil separators in surface water drainage systems*

Bibliography

SEPA/EA, 1999. *Sustainable urban drainage – an introduction*

HR Wallingford, 1981. *Wallingford Procedure*

The Stationery Office, various dates. *Design manual for roads and bridges*

The Stationery Office, 1998. *Manual of contract documents for highway works:*

– *Vol 1 – Specification for highway works*

– *Vol 2 – Notes for guidance of the specification for highway works*

– *Vol 3 – Highway construction details*